Jack *and* Jill
Are Over the Hill

Jack *and* Jill
Are Over the Hill

A Collection *of* Cockeyed Chronicles

Bonnie Willemssen

Copyright © 2014 Bonnie Willemssen

All rights reserved.

No part of this publication may be reproduced, distributed, or transmitted in any form or by any means, including photocopying, recording, or other electronic or mechanical methods, without the prior written permission of the author, except in the case of brief quotations embodied in critical reviews and certain other noncommercial uses permitted by copyright law.

ISBN-13: 978-1-505348-00-2
ISBN-10: 1505348005

Table of Contents

REGARDING RELATIVES..1
   Color My World...3
   Superwoman..7
   Mom's the Word...10
   Leftovers...13
   A Retired Husband is a Wife's Full-Time Job........16

TO AGE OR NOT TO AGE?...19
   Jack and Jill Are Over the Hill..............................21
   Mirror, Mirror on the Wall....................................24
   Ripe Old Age..27
   Younger Than Springtime......................................30
   Say Cheese...32
   Two Pees in a Pot..35

"WEIGHTING" TO WEIGH LESS..................................39
   What Doesn't Kill You Makes You Stronger........41
   To Sleep, Perchance to Dream..............................44
   KNEEd I Say More?..46
   What if the Sky Should Fall?.................................49

This Little Piggy Went to Exercise..................................52
Weight a Minute..54
Calendar Girl..57

Seasonal Celebrations..................................61
How to Host a New Year's Eve Party............................63
Poem For 2013..66
Step on a Crack, Break Your Mother's Back..................68
Rockin' Around the Christmas Tree in
My Wooden Rocking Chair..71
Who Gets to Take Home the Ring?..............................74
Ghosts and Goblins and Ghouls, Oh My!.....................77
Wherefore Art Thou Spring?.......................................80
Deck the Halls with Balled-up Holly............................83

Hodgepodge..87
Diary of a Bad Housewife..89
And, If I Am Elected...92
It's Raining Cats and Dogs..95
Retail Therapy..98
Small Town Fever...101
The Complete Idiot's Guide to Autos.........................104
The Great Outdoors..107
Have I Got A Deal For You!......................................110
Things That Go Beep In the Night............................113

Acknowledgements

This is the second book featuring humor columns I've written over the last two years. I want to thank my two editors, Diana Hammell of The Caledonia Argus and Dan Shearer of The Green Valley Sun and Times for allowing me to write for their newspapers. It's my great pleasure to work with both of them and I consider them friends.

I could not function without my friend and email buddy, Pat Poehling, who has tirelessly edited my essays BEFORE they go on to their respective newspapers. She says she loves to "correct me" and I appreciate it so much.

Jim, Ann and Erik, my family, have been such good sports when I feature them in my stories…without them, I'd have nothing to talk about. Thank you, Ann, for providing me with a grandchild so I will have even more fun and funny stories to tell.

Thank you, again, to Rob O'Byrne (Rob@jetlaunch.net) for doing a spectacular job of editing my work. And thank you to his wife, Debbie O'Byrne (Debbie@jetlaunch.net) for a great job of coordinating the cover of the new book with the cover of my previous book.

There are so many others to thank…friends who have listened to me read my essays over the phone (Mary Kroner) and friends who have read my ramblings and commented (Debbie Kramer) and to all the friends that felt obligated to buy my book 'cause they knew me….to them I say, get that charge card out again!

Thank you to everyone who enjoyed my previous book, Rocky Road is Not Just an Ice Cream. Your favorable comments have inspired me to compile Jack And Jill are Over the Hill. As my husband and daughter (who each have degrees in finance) would agree, it's good to be in the black, so I didn't publish this book till I "paid for" the last one. Me, I just write because it makes me happy to make others laugh.

Regarding Relatives

(If you can pick your nose, why can't you pick your relatives?)

Color My World

When I was young, my world was not very colorful. My house was *tasteful*; after all, my mother thought she was Martha Stewart—if Martha Stewart had been a celebrity back then—but, it was not *colorful*. Sheets were white, bedspreads were plain blue or green, rugs were a serviceable beige, and clothes were unexciting. But, when I was in 3rd grade, my mom brought home pink-striped sheets for my bed and my world changed forever. Pink-striped sheets! Was there anything more exciting in the whole wide world? Gradually, my world became more color-filled. Mom bought me a magenta sweater. I thought I looked like a million bucks in magenta. When I was in 8th grade my mom redecorated her bedroom. She went from the all blue ensemble to green drapes and bedspread with *lilac* flowers on the valence and the pillow shams. I wanted to spend every minute in that field of lilacs, and to this day it's my favorite flower.

My dad owned an office supply store in downtown La Crosse, Wisconsin. Each year before school started, he brought home the school supplies I needed. Fountain pens and ink wells (blue or black ink only), plain white tablets and mud brown folders, and a box of 48 Crayola crayons which of course I either broke, loaned out, or lost before the first month of school was finished. If you're close to my age, you may not have perused the office supply stores of today so you don't know you can get crayons in 200 count packages. Who could name 200 colors? Well, Crayola can. They have 'mini twistable' crayons so kids don't have to sharpen them—in colors like Frostbite and Absolute Zero no less. Hello, what color is frostbite? And zero usually means *nothing* in my mind. And have you bought markers lately? We didn't have markers when I was young. Now kids can use a chisel-tip fluorescent water-based smear-guarded marker in shades such as Café a Lait and Cerulean. And the kids know every hue. Of course, they can't remember to tie their shoes or where they parked their bikes.

How did this get so out of hand? How did we go from plain, ordinary, and simple to wild, vivid, and aromatic? Yes, aromatic. Crayons even smell like their names now. Do we really want young Janey and little Joey smelling *jelly beans* while they are supposed to be taking a spelling test? How about we just send them out for recess to smell real fresh air instead of having them use crayons that are *called* Fresh Air? We have gone from inhaling the mimeograph paper to writing our poetry on Lily of the Valley-infused pastel paper with fine-tipped calligraphic markers in Banana and Bubble Gum. I spent eons of time in the principal's office for chewing bubble gum. What would I have done with all that extra temptation in the form of my writing utensils? I'd still be reporting for detention now, between naps and filling out my Medicare card.

My mother was absolutely devastated that I had such a poor sense of taste in clothing choices. Left to my own devices I would have gladly put pink and purple socks with my moss-green plaid skirt and my lime-green blouse. Oh yes, in college I thought I was quite fetching in my hot pink dangle earrings, my apple-green shift and orange turtleneck. And when it got a little chilly walking across campus, I wore my fur-trimmed white boots. Ha! You kids really think you have the market cornered on UGGS, I mean *ugly*, footwear? Move over, darlings', I'm here to tell you that I give new meaning to the term *color blind*. Well, my mom probably thought I was color blind, but really I was color sighted. I loved color! All colors, all the time, all together. Poor Mom. My daughter, with the same discriminating taste as her maternal grandmother, looks me up and down when we are together and I see her thoughts in her eyes. Her mind is saying. "*Oh Lord. What in the world is she wearing now?*"

Once I had a party for my friend's *car*. It was really old and she was finally going to trade it in for a newer model. So I threw a "surprise funeral party" for the car and everyone was to come dressed in something they would never, under any circumstances whatsoever, wear to a funeral. My friend arrived. I answered the door with a flowered wrap-around skirt (remember those?) and a fluorescent-orange sweater. I dug out my hot pink earrings from college, and bought gold lame' chunky-heeled sandals from the Salvation Army. I put on panty hose full of runs (something I had handy as we wore panty hose all the time) and then added the *pièce de résistance*—about 15 strands of pearls. Meanwhile, my friend the car owner walks in and says not a word about my appearance. Later, I asked her if she wasn't suspicious when she saw the outfit I was wearing. She said, and I quote, "Not really, it just looked like something you normally wear." So, there you have it—a true testament to my suave and debonair manner of dress.

So if you see me in a restaurant or in the grocery store, and you suspect that I have dressed in the dark, please be kind and don't point out that my out-of-season white shoes do not match my burnt sienna slacks and my android-green top. You could compliment me on my earrings however, I'm sure they will look familiar—hot pink dangles from the '60s.

Superwoman

It's a bird, it's a plane, it's….just me. I always wanted to fly. Not in an airplane—far too scary! Nope, I wanted to fly just a few feet above tree level so I could scope out the neighborhood, searching for friend or foe, get a fix on my mother to avoid her "what are you doing wrong?" stare and plan my perfect touchdown to astound everyone. In hindsight, I realize I should have had loftier goals: get a piece of the moon for scientists to study (this was before men walked on the moon); find the Loch Ness monster and, most importantly, drop balloon bombs on those big bullies in the neighborhood.

Later I honed my super powers. When I taught third grade, I could "catch" students passing notes or poking their neighbor without turning from the chalk board. They were clueless that their reflection was in the glass doors of the bookcase. Later, I was the most informed mother with the best advice and the greatest ideas. Sadly, my elite status as *all-knowing mom cloaked in ever-blinking neon lights with sparklers flashing like a halo around her head* ended abruptly when my daughter entered teenage-hood. Suddenly I was the fuddy-duddy, hopelessly out of step, forever mired in non-coolness, incapable of uttering a word that didn't immediately reinforce my declining credentials as a *person of interest*.

Have you had that happen? One minute you were able to leap tall buildings in a single bound, and then, bang, you revert to cook, maid, garbage person, chauffeur, and calendar keeper and the role of adored superwoman slides to the back burner. Oops, I didn't mean to be sexist. You could just as easily have thought you were super*man* and felt those slings and arrows of outrageous indifference, too. Sorry not to afford you guys equal billing right from the get-go.

Are there any solutions to our common problem? Is the telephone booth gone forever? It very well might be, but, for the purposes of this column, let's suspend reality and remember that I'm writing in parody. The telephone booth is still there, you can still enter it, you can still change into your tighty-whities in relative anonymity, but, once you step out, it's not the clothes that make the man or woman, it's the attitude. And here is where you want me to tell you how my perception had an adjustment, and I'm now a hero to my daughter, a superwife to my husband, and the greatest person in the whole wide world. Well, I'm not going to say that. Are you kidding? Too much work. My super powers now consist of being able to sit absolutely motionless for two hours on the couch while I watch the boob tube.

Another of my super powers is being able to influence fashion styles when I buy a new outfit. Designers catch a glimpse of me in their duds and, horrified, immediately recall all similar couture and commence redesigning. I have also perfected the *fast food diet*. You eat all your meals at a fast food restaurant. After all, fast food means it goes through your digestive system so fast that you never absorb any of the calories. You don't believe me? Well, you should see me after several days on this diet; I am able to leap small pebbles in a single bound on my way to the restroom. Another of my super powers involves combining coupons in such a way that the establishment has to pay me to eat/shop there. I'm planning to give seminars on the topic. Day One: Careers in Coupon Clipping. Day Two: Beans and Bananas—a Budget Bargain. Day Three: Fudging the Finances and Finding Frugality. Day Four: Seven Secrets of Saving Shillings. Day Five: Galloping Gains in Grocery Guilt. I'm sure you will need to sign up early as these classes will fill quickly.

Okay, so I'm not Supermom. I probably never was. It was just a figment of my imagination. I do know that I have some good qualities. I brush my teeth twice a day, even when I'm tired; I haven't joined any secret organizations that want to subvert our government; I absolutely have never worn white after Labor Day, and only in case of extreme emergency would I ever let lutefisk touch my lips. So, what can I say, *super? Not super?* Supercalifragilisticexpialidocious? Oh good, I got a chance to work that word into a column.

Mom's The Word

You know what the worst part of motherhood is? It's not knowing which of your actions is going to screw up your kid. Will she be telling her therapist about the time you forgot to feed her turtle and told her it ran away from home? Or when you pretended your car broke down when really you had completely forgotten to pick her up from school? Maybe the thing she'll remember forever will be carry-outs eight days in a row when her dad was on a business trip?

When I was old enough to blame my *own* mother for everything that was wrong, screwed up or unsuitable about me, I decided I would raise my daughter totally the opposite of how my mother raised me. That meant never having an engraved-in-stone bedtime, clothing choices would be hers, and never ever would I make my child eat liver or sardines. Apparently there is a medical condition known as skip-a-generationitis because my daughter turned out to be everything my mother hoped I would be and I ended up raising my own mother. I wanted to put my little girl in jeans and sweatshirts because I was forced to wear frilly and feminine; my daughter begged for dresses. I hated having to practice the piano and performing; my daughter delighted in tickling the ivories and sparkled on the stage. My mom prayed to see me excel at something—anything—and my daughter did everything with honors. Lucky me!

Sandwiched between the two; daughter and grandmother—two peas in a pod; sophisticated, intelligent, inquisitive and self-motivated. Me? Not so much.

To make matters worse, my mother was a stupendous cook. She baked and fried and sautéed the most wonderful concoctions in the world but I was never allowed in the kitchen where I might screw up her system. When I married, I discovered that cooking was work. I mean, you have to read the recipe, go to the store to get the ingredients, schlep it all home, drag out the pots and pans, mix and fold and stir and blend, pour, bake, fry and freeze…and then, are you finished? Au contraire. Then you get to CLEAN UP!! Ladies, why are we cooking? Some smart lazy person invented restaurants where other people cook for you! My daughter, the gourmet, is appalled that my idea of fine cuisine is Taco Bell. She loves to eat in places with exotic sounding names that I cannot pronounce and if I could I would not eat there anyway because my philosophy is if you cannot pronounce a menu item, chances are you will choke to death on it.

So, it's scary to raise children. If you have more than one the odds are good that at least one of them will appreciate you, thank you for your dedicated service and reward you by having you come to live with them in your old age. However, I only had one and so there is no one to contradict her when she confides to the therapist that I made her scrub toilets from dawn to dusk and sleep in the cinders at night. No one to refute the statement that I made her shovel snow before walking six miles to school, or that I didn't remember to feed her for days. Well, that last may have been true. And here's the biggest fear of all—she'll write a *Mommy Dearest* book with me as the main character.

And the worst dagger in my heart will be when she accepts the Nobel Prize for singing the alphabet backwards or balancing the most Jenga pieces or inventing a robotic mother figure and reporters will ask her to credit who was most influential in her life. Will she remember all the times I sat outside the children's theatre waiting for rehearsals to be over? Or when I sat on the bench at tennis practice swinging my head back and forth and back and forth? Or my making dozens of cookies for pom squad practice? Or how about when I drove giggling, prepubescent girls to myriad ballet performances? Oh no. When she opens her mouth to name that important person in her life, me in the audience on the edge of my seat, ready to finally be recognized as MIM (Most Important Mom), the words that will come out of her mouth will be: "The person that most influenced my life was….."—*wait for it*—"My dad."

Leftovers

Thanksgiving is under our belt. One big meal gobbled up and then sliced, diced, and rehashed for days. It's not that I don't like leftovers; I do. My favorite memory of holidays past is supper on Thanksgiving Day and supper on Christmas Day. Mom would buy black rye bread, Braunschweiger sausage, Swiss cheese, and then there would be cold turkey and fruit—very German. She never heated leftovers that night; *heated* leftovers were for the next day. Dad had to have his sardines in the can (with their heads on), but I only had to eat one to satisfy my mother's demand that I try everything. Somehow sardines, liver, oyster stew and all that other slimy stuff never killed me, although if there were a Department of Child Abuse back then, I would have found a way to call them to report that my mother made me eat everything, no arguments allowed.

My husband Jim had the Norwegian influence of his mother for his holidays. They had lefse (the Norwegian way of making tortillas) and hot dishes (casseroles if you are not from the Midwest), cranberry steam pudding that was so sweet your teeth would fall out, and herring for Jim's dad. (Dads seem to be the same the world over). Creamed carrots and peas were always a staple at Thanksgiving and green bean hot dish for Christmas. I learned to embrace those traditions, too. Well, definitely not the herring—love and marriage can only go so far, after all. But, between my mom's Christmas cookies (gingerbread men, spritz, thumbprint cookies, rolled sugar cookies with colored sugar, and pecan roll-ups), and then Jim's mom's Christmas cookies (rosettes, krumkake, scrolls, Russian tea cakes and birds in a nest) I was in Nirvana, Shangri-La, Seventh Heaven, Valhalla and Never Never Land all rolled into one big basket of joy.

But, back to leftovers. Jim loves leftovers. He likes knowing that they are in the refrigerator and he can think all day about what he will mush together that night. He is not the least bit put-out if I don't cook for days because he can nurse leftovers like nobody's business. I tell people that Jim is always willing to scrape the mold off the mystery meat rather than throw it out. I am constantly trying to check our leftovers to make sure they still smell acceptable. "Jim," I'll say, "You cannot eat this. It's been four days and it looks greenish and it smells funny." He'll grab it, look it over, sniff it, and then say he'll eat it for lunch. So far we have not had an incident of *spoiled-food* poisoning so we have lucked out. Could I be charged for involuntary manslaughter? "Officer, I TOLD him not to eat it. I plead not-guilty by reason of HE NEVER LISTENS TO ME."

We know people that never take left-overs home. That's not the worst of it—Jim and I look at it with longing and express our disbelief that they are not taking that good pizza home for lunch they next day. Of course if they say, "Do you want it?" and we pounce like starving children from whatever country your mom told you children were starving in so that you would clean your plate. *It's a sin to waste food. Waste not want not. That's the way the cookie crumbles.* Whoops, that last one doesn't fit. So, as I was saying, we can't understand how someone could just throw away perfectly good food.

Being a person of the *no cooking* school of thought, I like to plan on how many days of leftovers there will be from any meal I prepare. Usually it's such an infrequent event that when Jim smells something emanating from the kitchen his first instinct is to call the fire department. Luckily we have not had to bother those wonderful, dedicated fire people because I've managed to stop him just as he has his finger ready to dial 911. That misunderstanding over, he then wrinkles his nose: "What do I smell?" he inquires suspiciously. "Well, really, it's not like I never cook around here you know," I say, insulted. "Yeah, it kind of is," he replies. Oh well, when he's right there's no sense arguing about it. I then outline the main meal, and just how our week will go: what will be frozen, what will be cobbled together with chicken broth into a soup, and what will be designated as the main part of our next three meals. It's an art to create four or five meals out of just one, you know. Don't laugh—it's my gift.

When it comes down to it, I guess the solution to leftovers is to just give everything a different name for each day you eat them. Thursday's turkey, mashed potatoes, gravy, broccoli, and candied sweet potatoes can be "Splendid Meat Mixed with Beige Liquid and White Puff" and then the next day it can be "Sweet Nothings over Verdant Green Veggies" and the last day it can be "Memorable Munching with Luscious Fruited Pâté'."

So, there you go, my secrets are revealed. Feel free to utilize my advice and copy me. I won't tell a soul. Belated Happy Thanksgiving.

A Retired Husband is a Wife's Full Time Job

Whether your husband is retired, getting ready to retire or years from retirement, listen to me carefully: Don't let him! Well, I guess you'll have to let him retire. After all, no one wants a 98-year-old window washer or an 87-year-old bulldozer driver or a 91-year-old plastic surgeon. So, there's the problem—the work force doesn't want them anymore and you have to allow them to come home and hang around 24/7. Think about that ladies. 24 hours a day and seven days a week Mr. Wonderful will be hanging around you. Here are some phrases you're sure to hear: "What do you need, dear?" "Can I help you with dinner, dear?" "Let me carry that for you, dear." Actually, that's just wishful thinking. You'll never hear those words and if you do, your hubby is probably afraid of you and to that I say: "Good job. How did you accomplish that?"

My husband is pretty good about keeping himself busy. He pays the bills, but unfortunately he then knows how much I spend and is happy to discuss the total of my restaurant excursions when the VISA statement arrives. He takes out the garbage, but has to point out that I forgot, yet again, to remove the tops from the water bottles and separate the glass and plastic correctly. He loves to help me grocery shop, but every time I stop to look at something on the shelf he asks me if it's on my list, to which I shout, "NO, AND WHAT'S IT TO YA?" Did you think I'd say, "No, dear, it's not? I'll put it back?" Ha! Like that would ever happen.

Jim loves spouting quotes. I know them by heart. One is: *Discretion is the better part of valor.* That means "Don't make me confront that big burley guy who just banged into our car". *What doesn't kill you makes you stronger.* I assume that means "If you don't remember to put gas in the car, don't come crying to me." *I'm finer than frog hair.* I've never been positive what he means by that, but I think it's a college term that has something to do with a biology class he eked through once.

So, how am I doin'? Did I capture *your* husband yet? Or is he one of those *wunderbar* spouses who does everything with panache and joy and a spring in his step like my neighbor who is such a great husband that he whistles while he works. Well, to be truthful, he's not retired so his wife doesn't have to spend every hour with him like I do with Jim. Is it any wonder that I belong to a knitting club, a Mah Jongg club, a lunch club, a book club, a garden club, and a valance of the month club (yes, I made that last one up).

Ladies, if you are young and have not yet let your husband develop bad habits, I have some advice. 1. Teach him to cook. You can thank me for that advice by mailing me food because I didn't teach my husband to cook and now I wish to retire from kitchen drudgery. 2. Teach him to vacuum. Don't let him plead that his back is bothering him. I finally had to *hire* someone to be the domestic goddess at our house. 3. Teach him to grocery shop. You won't ever get what you really want, in the sizes you hope for or the brands you need, but it will get him out of the house and you can put your feet up and watch TV. When he gets home, splash some water on your face, grab a dish towel and look harried. 4. Teach him to do laundry.

When I finally decided it was time for Jim to learn to wash our clothes, I came home to swirled pinkish clothes. I never asked again and wasn't he smart to "accidentally" ruin that load of tighty-whities? 5. Teach him to volunteer. It will be good for the community and helpful in your quest for peace and quiet. When your hubby is out volunteering, there are no sports on TV, no discussion of dwindling finances and, best of all, no helpful critiquing of what you are currently doing.

One last quote from my dear spouse: *Never get in a battle of wits with an unarmed person.* A lot he knows. Those are the arguments I can win.

TO AGE OR NOT TO AGE

(Do they offer a senior discount at the funeral home?)

Jack and Jill are Over the Hill

How can that be? Wasn't I just reading about those two little tykes scrambling up the hill after some liquid refreshments, and then tumbling down and running right back up that hill? The last hill I ran up was, ah, hummmm…have I ever run up a hill? There was a bluff I climbed once, but I walked, slowly and carefully, taking more time than Lewis and Clark took exploring the Missouri River. I'm more the sitting in my seat type, watching other people run up hills, like Tom Cruise in all twenty-eight of his Mission Impossible films. I figure they call them Mission Impossible because we ordinary non-hill-running-up type people could never do any of what we see in those movies. Personally I'm more of a Downton Abbey kind of person, preferring to call the servants to bring me my tea and let the mansion go to ruin while I send posts to my true love who is serving the Queen's Army in India.

My husband, who is three years older than I, loves to tease me about being over the hill. He makes fun of the fact that I bought an "authentic" Rolex watch for eight dollars in Mexico and it stopped just as I crossed the border. Apparently it's hilarious that I scout out every bathroom location from the moment we leave the house till we return. He complains that I snore like a stevedore now. When we were first married he thought it was cute that I snorted a little when I laughed. My memory is getting pretty bad. He gleefully reminds me that I can't remember what I was doing, where I was going, what I was saying, or to whom I told what. I tell him that the fact that we have to be in the restaurant for our "romantic" suppers by 4:30 PM means that he is *over the hill*, too. Also, when I'm making one of my many trips to the bathroom at night, I can't get back to sleep 'cause he's snoring like a pug—and that's not being kind to those poor LOUD pugs.

How did I get here? There was a time when I didn't tell stories about the past, 'cause the past was the present. That must be the problem—someone stole the present and that's why I live in the past. Oh how my father-in-law loved to tell tales of yesteryear. When I first started dating Jim, back in the era of dinosaurs and rotary dial telephones, his dad would start to tell a story of his childhood and pretty soon each of the six kids (Jim included) would slip away from the dining room table and skedaddle to another room so they didn't have to hear the retelling of yet another "walking through snowdrifts uphill both ways to school" story.

I have become my mother. And, yes, daughter of mine, you will become your mother, too, and I just hope I'm around for the day you hear yourself channeling me, or the day you quote your father's sage advice to your own children. Mostly I just want to live long enough to find out what the next modern fandangle inventions will be, the ones that will outdate things like Roku, Hulu, DVD, HBO, X-box, Smart TVs and Bluetooth. I want to hear my child complain because she feels slow, left-out, hopelessly lame-brained, and unable to grasp even the rudimentary essentials of communication with her children.

The other day I was shopping for swimsuits, a joy in itself. I checked my watch over and over to make sure I wasn't running late because my friend was going to pick me up later in the morning. In the middle of straining and swearing and sweating, while I pulled up a garment designed to contain an orca, I suddenly realized it had been 10:00 for a very long time. I checked my cell phone (yes, I've mastered the basics of cell phone ownership) and it was 11:30. I was being picked up ten miles away in thirty minutes. You think getting a swimsuit over this blubber is easy? Ha, try taking it *off* in a hurry. That requires the coordination of an

Olympic gymnast. But, dagnabbit, I made it home in time. So, don't call me *over the hill*, sonny. I'm in my prime—like a well-aged steak. Well, maybe not in my prime, but I'm well-preserved. Okay, that might be too strong a word.... how about hanging in there? I guess I'm really over the hill. But, you want to know what the best part of that is? I get to hop, skip and jump, (read: limp, hobble and fall) along the rest of the journey. I don't have to watch my p's and q's. I can speak my mind (what little is left), I can wear orange (what is that obsession old women have with purple?) whenever I feel like it, and best of all, if I want to eat bananas for supper and tacos for breakfast, I will.

I'll leave you with this little story about my mom. At the age of 91 she went to live in a nursing care facility. A few weeks later she whispered to me that she wanted to go home. I asked her why and she told me that there were all old people there. Half the people living there at the time were younger than she. To misquote a phrase: Age is in the eye of the beholder.

Mirror, Mirror on the Wall

I recently returned from a fleecing experience in Las Vegas, city of hustlers and those that get hustled. I'm the latter. Walking through Caesar's Palace, enjoying the beautiful Forum shops along the Appian Way, I wondered who these people were who could afford to shop in such extravagant elegance. A dress the size of a throw pillow listed at $3,200. Hot-pink (my favorite color) stilettos for a mere $860. I almost tried them on, but, no, I have an artificial knee, two creaky hips, an advanced case of vertigo, and early onset forgetfulness which could affect me adversely if I forgot I was wearing them.

As I continued to window shop, I saw diamond rings for $20,000 and matched lux leather luggage for only $4,295. Okay, enough about me sauntering along the cobblestone path, my jaw hanging open in wonder as I surveyed the fantabulous stores. I did notice that if it was skin tight, shorter than short, see through, and outrageous, someone was wearing it. They were both men *and* women, by the way.

A voice interrupted my reverie. "A sample, Miss?" Okay, I'll admit he had me at "Miss". His name was Chico and he drew me into his store, which was displaying classy cosmetics, exotic fragrances, and magical creams. He promised his products would make me look ten years younger. Ten years younger! That's nothing to sneeze at. I told him that obviously I was too young for these products now, but someday, way far into the future, I'd probably need them. Still, I was there. What did I have to lose? Except ten years, of course.

My mother called her facial treatment *vanishing cream* and I always thought some morning she would disappear. It took me years to figure out it meant that the wrinkles were supposed to vanish. So, when Chico flashed a smile that dazzled, I parked my ample rear on a creamy white faux leather stool, and thought, what the heck, I'll check out the new version of the old vanishing cream. And that's when the scraping and painting and scrubbing and remodeling began. In a unique plan of attack, Chico only worked with the right half of my face. This was so when he had me look in the mirror after a proper amount time for the concoction to work—two minutes—I would look in the mirror, compare my horribly disfigured left side (laugh lines, frown lines, wrinkles, and age spots) to the new and improved right half of my face. *EUREKA*, I would yell, tripping over myself as I ran to the cash register to buy this miraculous product! In reality I didn't see one iota of difference between the left and the right sides of my face. I kept looking (hoping) but, nope, nothing. Just plain old me.

"*No*," said I, "I don't need any of these." He informed me how important it was to protect my face, cleanse my face, moisturize my face, and slather my face—all for only $400.00. "You have beautiful eyes. I'll throw in the eye cream." *No, thank you.* "You are a nice lady; I'll add the night cream." *No, thank you.* "I want you to love our products so I'll include the facial scrub." *No, thank you.* "I'll give you the day cream, too." Admit it, you couldn't have resisted either. My Visa card moved from my purse to his hand. *Fait accompli.* I was paying $400.00 for creams I didn't need or want yet I smiled as I signed the receipt. Holy cow, how gullible can anyone be? Pretty gullible. It's amazing how the new vanishing creams work. You don't even need to put them on your face for your money to vanish in an instant.

Well, I've used the products every day for the last eight days. I'm sure that people who know me are doing double takes when they see me walk by. My friends are just being polite by not mentioning that they are amazed at how young I look. When I pick up my friend at the airport next week, she won't recognize me and will walk right past me, searching for her "old" friend. Please, if you see me, feel free to tell me, in the loudest voice you own, "BONNIE, YOU LOOK TEN YEARS YOUNGER."

So, mirror, mirror on the wall, who's the fairest of them all? Me! Me? Not!

Ripe Old Age

I've reached that ripe old age of, well, never mind what age I've reached, but know this: I have Medicare and Social Security on speed dial and the foaming mouths of nursing home insurance companies are nipping at my heels. My brown spots are multiplying as I write. The saggy skin below my face is really just a reminder of how important it is to eat enough food to "fill out" my pelican chin. My wrinkles could be laugh lines or frown lines but they are not adding to my charm or giving credence to my wisdom. They are just reminders that I am older than dirt and not likely to live to see the next millennium...or the next century...or maybe even the next decade...oh Lord, will I even see next Easter? I have so many wrinkles they've migrated into my ear canals and adhered to my brain, causing some problems with my memory. Who are all of you?

You know that icky smell of rotten apples or too-ripe bananas? Well, apparently someone must be adding it to my cologne. No matter what I buy it smells like Eau de Old. I tried a new fragrance last week and my husband spent the whole evening going around the house sniffing the garbage disposer, the wastebasket, and the drain in the sink, before finally declaring that a mouse must have died in the wall. I snuck into the bathroom to scrub off my new scent.

To add insult to injury, my legs look like a construction truck ran over them with studded snow tires. The Capri style pants (pedal pushers for those of you that are my age) are not flattering with bulging veins, flabby calves and puffy ankles. What happened to my assets? What happened to my youth? Who sidetracked me on my way to being sexy and sophisticated? I pictured myself winning MORE Magazine's best preserved model of the year award. I waited for them to call for weeks but alas, no call came. How did I not win with all my wonderful attributes like thin hair, white hair, chin hair, nose hair, eyebrow hair, fallen hair, hair in the drain—oh, sorry, I got carried away there…with hair.

Also, I guess I need to mention my butt. It's ginormous. I mean, just trying to find a pair of jeans to cover my nether region is *Mission Impossible*. And if the jeans fit over my gluteus maximus and actually cover my jello-like tummy, then you can be sure some idiot designed the pant legs to fit like nylon stockings over the bulges of my thighs. (Do these designers ever even *look* at fat people?) And, once the bottom half of me is successfully covered in a tummy control, buttocks control, and thigh control pair of pants, I have to work on the top half. Short sleeves are not allowed in my world. I could be lost in the desert, in 200 degree weather, no breeze and no water for miles, and I would still keep on my long-sleeved top because I wouldn't want anyone who rescues me to see the perpetual jiggle of my underarms. Why doesn't someone make girdles for arms? I might have to invent it myself and put it on eBay.

So, once I'm covered from my multiple necks to my little piggy toes with loose, non-clingy clothing, there is the application of accessories. I love accessories. Shoes are easy and purses and jewelry are one-size-fits-all. And don't you love pashminas (shawls for those of you that don't speak Himalayan goat)? With a pashmina there are no too-tight sleeves and no buttons that don't meet in the middle. Accessories are a "fluffy" lady's mecca and I'm so darn fluffy that most clothing does not fit me. I have to shop in the *super big mama* store and the local tent and awning company.

Years ago, when I was stick thin, I laughed at the word diet, scoffed at the word exercise, ridiculed the word lettuce and jeered at the word metabolism. Unfortunately, the god of calories worried I'd spiral into anorexia and decreed he would fatten me up. Obviously, I've not been able to thwart his powerful curse, so I've been doomed to live my life with lumps and bumps and ripples and jiggles. I do have one last comment—it's not over till the fat lady eats the last cherry cordial.

Younger Than Springtime

Yup, that's me, younger than springtime. Think about it. Springtime. The season has had hundreds of thousands of birthdays. Every single year, on March 21, spring comes rolling in. Even before a bunch of Mayans or Gregorians invented the calendar, even before Guinevere danced and sang "Tra la! It's May," springtime was having her birthdays. So, when I say I'm younger, I haven't beaten her by much and I feel every moment of my advanced years. First, there is spring cleaning. That's a lot of work for a devoutly committed lazy person such as I. Writing out the list of chores is taxing and my poor fingers cramp for hours. And good grief, how my shoulders ache from all the weeding and gardening I direct my husband to do. I point and gesture so much I am unable to lift my arms to comb my hair, and that's the excuse I use for why it looks like a group of rabid beanie babies made their home atop my head.

I look around the house and realize a rummage sale is in order. Boy, does the clutter accumulate. It really doesn't seem like spring unless you clean out the garage, does it? Naturally, when I say *you*, I mean *you and my husband*, not me. I can barely open and close my jaw after giving orders about where all the junk, oops, I mean treasures, should go in the garage.

I'm on a spring fever kick. Well, I'd like to kick spring fever right in its…oh, sorry, I got carried away there. I bought walking sticks for my annual "It's spring and I better get my act together and lose weight before I have to shed my parka and mukluks" tradition. My philosophy on exercise is that it should always be rewarded with treats – it's my "good dog" theory. I'm pretty sure I invented it. And, if at any time, my exercise routine gets waylaid—you know, a grizzly bear standing outside my door in the morning, or a call that I won the Publisher's Clearing House Sweepstakes, or I look through the window and see it's raining, snowing, misting, sleeting, blowing, sunning or any of those other things that happen *outside*—then my alternative is that four-letter word: *diet*.

My mom and dad, bless their hearts, worked very hard. You'd think it would have rubbed off on me. Mother cooked everything from scratch and Dad worked all day in his store and came home to yard work. Whew. Maybe it was seeing how hard they worked that cured me of any desire to emulate that behavior.

As I close this missive, I am reminded that I am certainly not younger each year when spring comes calling. You would think after all this time spring would know not to show up when there is still snow on the ground, and when it's blustery and icy, and when lilacs and lily-of-the-valley are far from showing their faces. I, at least, know to hibernate until all traces of winter have faded. I have discovered that pre-spring headquarters are located inside. Windows were invented to check on winter's departure and spring's appearance, and there is this wonderful invention called central heating. April showers bring May flowers? Hurry up!

Say Cheese

I heard that the lady who takes our driver's license photos is retiring. Thank the Lord! My last license had the *wrong* woman's photo on it. It showed some *old dame* with white hair and several chins and wrinkles on top of wrinkles. How could anyone ever think that was me? I marched right back to the desk to have her redo it, but she said it looked just like me. *What? Wait a minute. I know I have long, blond tresses, I'm pencil thin, and my skin is as smooth as a soft serve ice cream cone.* To add insult to injury, somewhere some lucky lady has *my* picture on *her* license and she's not complaining at all.

I seem to always have problems with photos of myself. I needed my passport renewed, and the only background allowed in the U.S. is white. I requested a more flattering color and they would not budge. I guess if you have a red background, they think you are from Russia and a blue background must be only for Icelanders and green apparently means you are Irish. Who knew? Anyway – America has a white background, and since my hair is white (I know, I fibbed in the first paragraph), I look like I have NO hair in the picture. It's just a face. I don't even look bald – which could be kind of a cool Kojak look. Remember Kojak and his lollypops? No? Well, then please pass this column on to your parents.

My mother took all the pictures in our household. Dad and I suffered in silence while she set up her tripod, attached her camera, adjusted the lenses till we were focused, and then we would look at the camera, smile, stand up straight, say cheese and snap...the darn flash bulb didn't work! When mother picked up the pictures a week later from the camera shop, she would complain bitterly that she never ended up being in any of the pictures and she'd look accusingly at my father. Next holiday, my dad would gamely offer to take a photo of her. She would act modestly surprised: *"What? You want little ole' me in the picture? Oh, well, if you really insist."* Then the process would begin again, but this time she would step out from behind the camera after she had it focused and take her place, front and center. My dad would click. When mother brought home the pictures, she'd be nowhere in that little glossy square...because my dad invariably pushed the wrong button, or had his finger over the lens or jostled the camera out of focus. You don't want to know the conversation that ensued. Eventually she bought a Polaroid camera so at least we knew in five minutes if the picture-taker goofed up or not.

Despite my early experiences with a rabid photo bug, I decided to record the important moments of our lives when Jim and I married. I'd take pictures of our garden, the front of our house, our new car and then discover I had no people in my life journal. New goal: get more people in my photos...easy peasy with self-focusing cameras. The next few years I photographed every person we encountered...the mailman, the dog groomer, the girl who made my popcorn at the movie, the guy who cut the meat at the deli—well, he was cute so I might have had other reasons to include him in my photo montage. On our 25th wedding anniversary I looked through our old photograph albums. Who in the heck were we with on the sandbar? Who was eating at the restaurant with us? Did we really know a couple who both had carrot red hair? And, please, surely we didn't hang out with three gals who all dressed alike but weren't triplets? I spent the next few months culling through old photographs and eliminating the ones with no people and the ones where we couldn't name the people in them.

Photographs are really precious. They are a record of your life, of the person you were and the person you have become. The good news: everyone has a camera with them on their cell phone. The bad news: now someone might photograph me picking my nose! Say cheese!

Two Pees in a Pot

Author's note: No words were misspelled in the writing of this title. Here's a typical day in the life of a middle-aged (ha, like you believe that) writer.

7:00 a.m.: It's morning and something disturbs my slumber. Oh right, it's my bladder yelling at me to get out of bed *now* and get into the bathroom or there will be hell to pay (translation: sheets to change). I open my eyes to mere slits so no light wakes me further. Later, I limp back to bed (bad knees) and crawl between the sheets again. The open window is letting chilly air in. What happened to those lovely summer breezes from the night before? I snuggle under the blanket, shivering. *Go back to sleep, darn it!* Then, just when I've drifted into sweet dreamland, my husband bounds in to discuss the day. He's already exercised, read the paper, had breakfast and watered the lawn. Have I ever mentioned how much I *hate* morning people? I am sometimes in bed as early as midnight, which is at least two hours later than my life partner who usually is snoring before the news starts. It's a joy to be married for 42 years to a guy who springs out of bed at the crack of dawn. Okay, okay; neither of us is probably ever going to change.

9:00 a.m.: Despite my efforts to ignore him, Jim's running commentary about everything under the sun has disturbed my sleep enough that I have to scurry to the bathroom. I might have a lovely eight hours of sleep if I didn't get up three times to go the bathroom and if I didn't have my C-PAP breathing tube attached to my nose through the night. Sometimes, just for fun, it tries to strangle me, and now and then it gets pulled from my face which precipitates a resounding snap. Okay, Okay, I'm *up*!

11:00 a.m.: Gee, I'm ready to take a nap. I've been up for hours. Well, two hours. Isn't it naptime yet? I've made the bed, I've gotten dressed, I've eaten breakfast and I'm at the computer writing my column. I'm icing my knee 'cause it hurts and this is my "good" knee. The other one is my bionic knee, replaced almost two years ago. Just as I get comfortable, computer on my lap, iced tea at my hand, pillow at my back, I realize that I have to go to the bathroom again.

1:00 p.m: Lunchtime. I've studied and perused the contents of the refrigerator and cupboards for fifteen minutes and neither of them yielded a whit of promise. I crave carbs, of course, but I've purged the house of bad carbs, whites (sugar and flour) and candy is a no-no. *Sigh*. I bring my hot vegetable (read: healthy) soup to the table. I proceed to spoil it with tons of salt, and just as I am ready to dig in…Mother Nature calls. She is very insistent and will not let me ignore her. I have to leave the table and when I return my soup is cold. They say you should be mindful of what you eat and not read or watch TV while you are consuming food. I say just the opposite; when you're on the cardboard and paste diet (soon to be on bookshelves everywhere) it's best to distract yourself while you grimace with every bite.

3:00 p.m.: Finally I can officially take a nap. I've been waiting all day for this guilty pleasure. You're thinking that if I didn't nap I'd get to sleep earlier, but I take this nap so I can stay up later. I start to come alive late at night. My adrenalin begins pumping, my creative juices start flowing, my fingers fly over the keyboard and no one is around to see the Oreos I munch while I work. Only one problem plagues me when taking a nap; long before I'm ready to lift my head from the couch pillow I've slumped against, I have to go to the bathroom. Did you guess that?

5:00 p.m. until midnight: Did you think I was going to run through my entire day in two hour increments? Well, I was, but I'm running out of space for my column… unless you want a two-parter? So, meanwhile back at the ranch, I cook a scrumptious meal for my husband, not imbibing in the repast myself because of my adherence to my, well, for want of a better word, unappealing diet. We watch hours of our favorite shows—whoever said too much togetherness is not healthy was wrong. At least, that's what I'm saying on paper. After all, my husband reads my column, too! I drink copious amounts of water while watching these shows because water is good for me and I spend a lot of commercials in the loo. That's what commercials are for. I told my mother that when I was about six years old. It's still true.

Some people mark the passing of time by birthdays, some by the turning of pages of the calendar, others by their weekly phone call from children/grandchildren; I mark the passage of my minutes, hours, days, weeks, months and years by the rolls of toilet paper that parade into our house so frequently.

"WEIGHTING" TO WEIGH LESS

(Shouldn't EL GRANDE be a dress size?)

To Sleep, Perchance to Dream

It came as a shock that a sweet, delicate flower such as I was snoring like a stevedore and driving my husband nuts with my nocturnal symphony. That fact, combined with my daytime exhaustion, drove me to a sleep professional. I carefully skewed my pre-appointment questionnaire to paint me in the best light. During the appointment I glossed over anything that could result in an overnight stay, but I blew it when I claimed my memory was perfect and then couldn't remember the name of my internist. Busted!

A Health Alert for you, my readers: apparently not sleeping well causes strokes, heart attacks and other maladies. To prove it's less scary than the Bates Motel, the clinic shows prospective non-breathers a video of someone with forty wires glued to his head, face, and legs. I am sure in the battle of me against a C-PAP mask, I would lose and forever have elastic marks across my cheeks. Reluctantly, I arrived for my overnight sleep study at 7:30 P.M., tired. They told me I could wear what I *normally* wore to bed. Ha, like that was going to happen! What if they videotape me kicking off the covers and everyone sees my granny panties! I told my friend I was worried they'd use my sleep video at the office Christmas party. She said that's the least of my worries—worse would be that it could end up on YouTube.

The technician told me I would be awakened at 6:00 A.M. to go home. I told her that that wasn't possible, as I don't get up till 9:00 A.M. She assumed I was joking! Wrong.

I waited with the other sleep study candidates, all of us forced by our spouses to get *fixed*—or else. My room had a private bath, a TV, and wires and machines everywhere. I had changed into my footed PJ's when I heard a voice speaking to me from the ceiling. "Are you ready, Bonnie?" "Yes, Lord," I answered. *Wow, God is a woman*! Ok, it wasn't the Lord, but that would have made one heck of a next column, right?

Next they attached all the wires that convey information that tells the doctors if I need to be forever hooked to a device to help me sleep. The electrodes are attached by a combo of glue, cement, spit, and ether. Yes, ether. If you've ever had surgery in the old days, you'll remember the smell. They make sure those pesky electrodes won't come off in the night. Then, in the morning, they jackhammer them off. Kidding! However, I now know where they recruit people to electrocute convicted murderers…they hire retired sleep study technicians.

Once in bed, I could read or watch TV, but no getting up without an assistant. I was sure I slept like a log, but my poor technician had to stay awake all night. I know this because my cell phone rang once (I forgot to turn it off. Don't you hate people that do that?), I had a hunger attack and absolutely, positively needed to eat something, I spilled my water bottle that sat next to my bed, and I had to go to the bathroom twice. Each incident required that the technician come in and unhook my wires, wait for me to complete my tasks, and then hook me up again.

The next morning they removed the glued electrodes by a similar, stinky-ether process. When I left, I had pieces of dried glue hanging from my face and hair and people gave me a wide birth, assuming that I had leprosy. I pretended that I was trying out my "Night of the Living Dead" Halloween costume.

The results of my study took weeks to analyze. After all, they had to comb through eight riveting hours of *Bonnie's Bedtime Boondoggle*. Did I pass? Did I fail? I could hardly sleep waiting for the results, which is kind of poetic, don't you think? Alas, I was positive I would be given the bum's rush after my doctor met with me, but, wrong again. Apparently if you stop breathing five times in an hour, it's considered normal. I so aspire to be normal. If you stop breathing fifteen times in an hour they consider you a candidate for the gas mask, I mean, the C-PAP mask, and if you stop breathing thirty times in an hour you are dead. Just kidding! My number was 28. Yikes. Didn't have a clue. And yippee, I get to wear that sexy mask. Problem solved.

Note: I've been using the C-PAP machine for several months now and it's fine. I don't mind it a bit. I hardly notice it's even there. My 'stop breathing numbers' have dropped to .5 times per hour, which is great, and my husband is happy that he doesn't have to smother me with a pillow to stop me from snoring.

KNEEd I Say More?

As a result of my absolute abhorrence to exercise, I'm in a pickle. I need to have a total knee replacement. I read that millions of people have knees replaced each year. I imagined I'd be a foxy middle-aged dame, tall (did I think I'd grow taller?), well dressed (as opposed to the sweats I live in now), and *thin* (I haven't been thin since the Nixon years). To me the perfect blend of health and exercise activities is called THE BUFFET; it combines weight lifting (filling your plate to the brim) and aerobics (getting up for seconds, thirds, and, of course, the dessert corner).

 I was minding my own business, trying to walk off the accumulation of fat since those Nixon years, when I felt a twinge of pain in my left knee. My inner self told my outer self to *ignore it*! That was my first mistake. Not in my whole life, but certainly in the last week or so. Who knew walking through the pain was not a good choice? I was forced to admit that I might have a knee problem and the specialist agreed. Well, there was no way I was going to have my knee operated on and, after several "ass over tea kettle" falls, I started to use my cane to steady myself. You know how pregnant women are like a homing device for people to pat their tummies? Well, my cane seems to be the homing device for people to tell me about their knee replacements. I bit the bullet and made an appointment for the operation. Darn, I guess other people want their knees replaced too, 'cause I had to wait my turn. Fine.

I will have to be "put under" for my surgery. That is scary. Drifting off into la-la land and knowing nothing about what's going on in the outside world. Who cares about the outside world? I just want to know what's going on in *my* operating room. Did they notice the purple magic marker writing on my right knee saying "wrong knee"? Are they discussing the layers of blubber they have to go through to get to my knee? Are they laughing at how my fat flows over the sides of the operating table? Are they discussing the latest football game or who is next to be voted off *Survivor*? I'm going to tell them I've hidden a tape recorder on my person somewhere and I'm going to be playing it back at a later date. I don't know why I can't be awake for this procedure, anyway. I could keep them entertained by reading some of my columns to them. Well, maybe not. I don't want their raucous laughter to interfere with steady hands and steely determination.

So, wish me luck. I'll let you know about the gory details after I'm home and recuperating. I hear you get a video of the procedure – I'll lend it out. I know you will want to view it with friends and family.

Last thought. I do not want any visitors in the hospital. I am sure when you see me at the farmer's market, you gaze in wonderment at my polished beauty. You, of course, assume it's au naturel. I assure you, I spend hours in front of the mirror each day to get my face on, my hair perfect, and to find the best outfit (meaning anything that fits over my fat behind). I don't want you to see what I really look like when I roll out of bed at the crack of ten o'clock each day. That would be horrifying for both you and me.

NOTICE: I have OCD. If you come to visit me in the hospital I'm quite sure I will die of germaphobia. The hospital will have a big inquest into my death. Heads will roll! And it will be all because you came to visit me. Stay home and send me an e-mail. A friend of mine told me she had a visitor come trippin' in while she was sitting on the bed pan. That's the stuff from which nightmares are made.

What Doesn't Kill You Makes You Stronger

As you read this missive I will be five weeks and one day post-surgery. Holy cow—what a lot of pain and agony and well, frankly, *work*. I go to physical torture (that's what PT stands for, you know) three times a week where Genghis Khan and Attila the Hun work me over with rubber hoses. Okay, it's not *that* bad, but physical therapy is not for wimps. I really only have two choices. 1) Don't do the therapy and walk like a peg-legged pirate forever or 2) Do the therapy, but curse and scream till my neighbors are forced to move. I don't even want to know what might be behind door number three.

I digress. I want to tell you about someone special—St. Jim. I know you can't even imagine it's my husband I'm talking about. Yes, it's the very same Jim I use for all my jokes and stories—poor maligned Jim. Well, let me tell you, that guy stepped up to the plate and hit a home run. He has been my cook, my cleaner, my shopper, my chauffeur, my dish washer, my telephone answerer, my physical therapist in residence, and my pal these last five weeks. He has had to spend 24/7 with me. Lord, what a chore that is. Normally I'm out and about attending to breakfast, lunch, Mah Jongg, or shopping duties. Sometimes I don't see him from morning till night. He's had to listen to me moan, groan, grumble, and cry. He's had to watch me stumble, wobble, lurch, and flounder. Next time you see him, pat him on the back. He deserves it.

If you are contemplating knee replacement surgery, I might not be the best one to give you a deciding vote. I'm not far enough along to be glad I did it. But I do improve every day, so, I know I'll get to that point. My sister-in-law had a second knee replacement about 2 months after the first. THAT I cannot imagine. I'm going to have to be about five or ten years down the road and drunk as a skunk before I decide I'll go through this again. And don't forget, you all know me pretty well now—I'm lazy as a slug; I don't like pushing a broom, so why would I like pushing my knee to make it bend properly? Apparently the best outcome for a knee is to get to 120 degrees, which is normal. Yikes. I don't see why a person has to go over 100 on anything. In my school years, if I ever would have gotten 100 on a test my mother would have fainted, and I would have ridden on that glory for a whole decade. So when they say 100 is not good enough, I think, "Well sprinkle me with sugar and call me a donut." Who ever heard of a system like that? I'm not one to question the wisdom of the ages, but this knee business is a bit too complicated. I wonder if God anticipated that someday they'd be replacing things like hips and knees and ankles. Back when we were all happily cavorting in the Garden of Eden, I think everyone's joints worked pretty well. I blame the snake! Darn him!

I have friends getting ready for their own epic journey through knee replacement surgery. I'm trying to give them all the pearls of wisdom I've accumulated as the advance woman for this procedure. Here are my suggestions: Take all the drugs they give you for as long as they let you. Beg, borrow or steal at least ten canes; you will need them in every room in your house because they work great for lifting your leg on and off the couch or bed. Get handrails for the commode; take up all your loose rugs or you might be going back quickly for more surgery. Take more drugs. Lay in a supply of food to last for several months or as long as you think you can keep claiming you are 'recuperating'. Allow everyone and their brother to wait on you hand and foot, especially when they offer to bring your drugs over to you with a nice glass of water. Don't plan to drive for six weeks so make sure all your neighbors are on the alert and that your spouse, if you have one, is ready to give up life as he or she knows it for the foreseeable future. Take more drugs. That's it. All my advice. Well, I might have missed a few key things, but don't forget, I am on drugs. I just signed up for a triathlon and for some reason Jim won't send in the registration check. I guess he thinks I might need a little more therapy. Where are those drugs?

What if the Sky Should Fall?

~~~

Six years ago I was diagnosed with OCD. My first thought: *Yikes, I have a disease with initials? Is it a brain-eating virus? Will I be banished to the island of Molokai?* Visions of me sitting in a nursing home, drool dribbling down my chin, flashed through my mind. Obsessive Compulsive Disorder? Me? The doctor must be wrong! After all, don't most people wash their hands twenty-two times a day? Who in their right mind would let dishes pile up in the sink, leave magazines unaligned on the coffee table or allow pillows to languish willy-nilly on the couch? Life is better when things are straightened and arranged and orderly and systematic and regulated and legislated and managed and governed and stabilized and columnized and calendarized. Oh dear, maybe one of the symptoms of OCD is getting carried away with adjectives.

Maybe I overreacted *slightly* when I first heard my diagnosis. I know that Molokai is now a lovely resort destination and nursing homes are practically like spas these days. I could cope. Besides, I always laughed at my idol Adrian Monk, the neurotic star of the TV series, *Monk*. No way was I as bad as he. Well, apparently I was *exactly* like him. When he would straighten a picture in the dentist's office or wash all his clothes after walking in the park, I never understood why that seemed weird to others. Monk was this perfectly normal guy doing what people should be doing—protecting themselves from the bombardment of germs, air borne pathogens, viruses, hoof and mouth disease, and that mutation that makes people want to wear purple. OCD has been a part of my life for so long that it all seems normal to me. I always assumed everyone felt and acted the way I did, but apparently other people are not blessed with the compulsion to tidy the placemats, salt and pepper shakers, catsup and mustard bottles, bud vases, silverware and glasses at their table in the restaurant. I should get credit for my self-control; I don't do that to *every* table. I think restaurants should be thanking me for the improvements I make. You're probably wondering how I can eat out in the first place when I can't be sure of the direction of a sneeze. And just what does go on behind those swinging doors of which we only get a glimpse? I guess when it comes to someone cooking for me vs. me having to cook, I'm able to keep some unpleasant images at bay.

I am a tad obsessive about various things in my life. A dead giveaway is my car in which you can always find a sweater, gloves, ear muffs, umbrella, comb, makeup, coin purse, mints, gum, salt shaker, artificial sugar packets, water bottles, Band-Aids, Purell, tennies, emergency earrings, deodorant, sunglasses, and a book. Oh, and toothpaste. I never know when I might have to stay overnight somewhere between the mall and my house.

Part of OCD is the "what if" syndrome. What if the sky should fall? What if there is a hurricane, a tornado, a rain storm, a flood, a triple-digit day, a sudden downpour that messes up my hair, a traffic jam that forces me to wait for hours, a close encounter with a sales person when my breath isn't minty fresh? What if my car breaks down and I have to walk twenty miles to the nearest gas station? Sure, I'm a member of AAA and I have a cell phone, but what if the cell tower gets struck by lightning and AAA goes out of business that morning? And the restaurant could be too cold, and what if they ran out of salt, my favorite condiment, and did I mention it could rain? Okay, it's a little burdensome living with OCD, but it's my reality.

There's another problem that OCD sometimes accelerates — the "if only" syndrome. If only I had done *this* differently. If only I had made *that other* choice. If only I had been better at ____ (fill in the blank). The perceived mistakes of my past swirl around in my mind constantly, often accompanied by tears despite telling myself that I made the best choice I could make <u>at the time</u>. With OCD I am always trying to keep one step ahead of my own warped perception of what might happen or what did happen and there is no time to analyze the irrationality of my thoughts and behavior. I barely keep ahead of my idiosyncrasies. I try to laugh at myself when I can't help performing such weird behaviors and I playfully tell people that I'm anal-retentive and they laugh, too. I hope no one notices that even though the lights have flashed and the horn has beeped, I am compelled to try the handle three more times to make sure the car door is locked.

My doctor used the words, "Suffering from the condition of OCD." Suffering? I tried to explain to her that having this condition is a blessing. I told her my house is so clean I could invite anyone to stop over anytime…and eat off my floors, visit my perpetually ready guest bedroom and check out my sparkling bathrooms. Should you choose to open a cupboard—well, please don't do that. I still have a couple "normal" cells in my brain that allow me to hide the clutter inside the drawers and closets!

This Little Piggy Went to Exercise

I am going to talk about a topic that few people want to mention in polite company. It's usually discussed behind the closed door of your doctor's office or perhaps over a few too many cosmos at a bridal shower, but now, out into the open it must be. I am going to discuss, are you ready? EXERCISE. What, you talk about it all the time? You say you don't think it's a dirty word? You indulge in *exercise* a lot? Well, throw me in the fire and call me a marshmallow, I guess I'm always the last to know. My furtive forays into this metabolism boosting activity have been done under the cloak of darkness with a trench coat and sunglasses worn to protect my anonymity. Now, you're telling me that some people actually go to places like gyms and dance studios? Wow. And those people I see on the sidewalks are not going to a store, they're going up and down and around and around so that they can get fit and firm? Do tell.

Okay, I'll let you in on a little secret. I've tried exercising over the years. I've been seen at the gym often. Well, maybe not often, but sometimes. Okay, not that much, but people know my face. They say things like, didn't you come here once three years ago? Gosh I hate people with good memories.

Last year I found a place where people do things that are kind of kinky but, as you perform the tasks required of you, those kinks melt away. Meltaways…yum, those sound good. The activity I paid to endure is called Pilates and for someone whose muscles never lifted more than a diet cola, it was quite challenging. First they lure you there by saying you will be lying down on a bench. That can't be too hard, right? (When I got there I found out the bench is called a "reformer" and I should have heeded my inner voice that said *run*.) The instructor asks you to hold your legs in a *tabletop position* and in seconds your stomach muscles are screaming, "Hey, a little help down here."

When I convey to the instructor that I'm not in good enough shape to do the basics, my punishment for insubordination is to add more time and reps to my routine. Meantime, my stomach is not happy. Before I can tell them how I had a C-section only thirty-five years before, I'm being directed to breathe through my nose and do three hundred (well, maybe only ten) sit ups and I'm not to dare use that tempting bar over my head for help because the punishment for that infraction is to add ten more of whatever I'm attempting to do. They evaluate your walk and evaluate your strength…ha, I can't lift *anything*. I'm sure I was the bane of their existence, or maybe they were secretly pleased I was such a wonderful lump of clay with which to work. Michelangelo should have been so lucky. I went two or three times a week for torture, I mean, ah, strengthening. I did whine a lot though, which I'm sure they found charming.

Someday, when I'm old and gray….Oh okay, I'm already old and gray now so I guess I'll just say; Someday, I'll be strong, healthy and fit because of my pursuit of all things active. This year it's water aerobics. It's been great. Except I have to get up at the crack of 7:15 to make it to the pool early enough to claim a good spot to jump and hop and push and pull and make a lot of noise, which apparently, according to the instructors, gets our metabolisms going. I hope to stick to this program longer than all the ones of the past. Historically speaking, I'm an exercise dropout, so as soon as I buy new shoes, bake a cake, learn to paint, clean the bathroom, return that book to the library, call my friend, and win the lottery, I'll be completely ready to devote my full attention to nothing but honing my body into an instrument of power and perfection. I think I'll start…TOMORROW.

Weight a Minute

Do you know that the human body gets larger in space? The longer an astronaut is up there the larger his/her body gets. Can I get my deposit back on that Mars Mission I signed up for? I thought we would be weightless in space—I like that idea—and I was hoping they might perfect that phenomenon and we could be weight-*less* back here on earth. But, larger? I think not! I suppose a 90 pound weakling might want to book a trip to Jupiter or Venus, but, for us plus-sized persons, getting larger is not our goal. I guess I'll stay on earth and find a way to keep from getting larger without going the opposite way and becoming too thin. Well, the likelihood of me getting too small is akin to the earth and the moon colliding or George Clooney riding up to my door on a white steed. Can you picture it? George reaching for my hand to help me up and me pulling him right off the horse, the horse trotting off, neighing gratefully that he didn't have me on his back.

People have all kinds of weight loss systems that work for them. For instance, my mother was a great seamstress. To facilitate her sewing needs, she had a mannequin made to her exact body measurements so she could use it to make dresses. I am positive that is why Mother never gained or lost a pound in her lifetime. On her 60th wedding anniversary she put on her wedding gown, and it fit—perfectly. Ladies, having a mannequin made to your measurements might be the best diet trick ever. Matter of fact, why not have it made to the measurements you wish you had?

Unbelievably, some clothing companies have size zero as one of their sizes. Size zero! Who the heck is a size *zero*? Wouldn't you have to be invisible to wear a size zero? And then, why bother to wear any clothes at all? I say, go naked; it's cheaper. And are you even allowed to eat if you are a size zero? I want my comfort foods; I have no desire to lose weight if it means giving up my favorites: pizza, coconut cream pie, pizza, oh, I said that, movie popcorn, cream of *anything* soup (emphasis on the cream), bread, butter, bread, butter, bread, butter, cheese, cheese, cheese. If you notice a certain lack of veggies and fruits, you may ascertain as to why I'm plus-sized and not zero-sized.

If you're like me, you may have tried a few dozen (hundred) different diet plans over the years. The "tape your mouth shut" diet, the "wire your jaw shut" diet, the "wear catchers mitts at meal time" diet, the "encircle your refrigerator with duct tape" diet, the "lock yourself in the exercise room" diet. Yup, I've tried them all. And nope, none of them worked for long. It's called yo-yo dieting. After a while you get pretty good at it. The steps to being a great yo-yo dieter is as follows: lose weight, buy new clothes, give away oversized clothes, gain weight, buy new clothes, and give away too small clothes. It's great stimulus for the economy, and you're providing for the less fortunate at the same time. It's practically noble.

You would think that as much as I like to talk when I go out to eat with friends, I would lose weight. I take a bite here, tell a story, a bite there and tell more of the story. Soon my food is cold, but I need to finish my story. Meantime, the others at the table are finished, have paid their bills and are gathering their purses. Is it something I said?

My motto is POTATO CHIPS ARE MY LIFE. Does that about sum it up for you? If only the things I love would love me back by being good *for* me. Have you noticed that? How all the good stuff we love has too much fat, too many calories, too many carbs, and too many sugars? Of course if it's good for you, like celery, then you can eat all you want, but who the heck wants to?

You know that old cliché "I'm too short for my weight?" It's true. Actually, my weight would be perfect for me if I was seven and a half feet tall. Then I'd look like Miss Twiggy instead of Miss Piggy.

Calendar Girl

January first and the snow is around; my big tummy still drags on the ground.

January second and I'm out of shape; too big for a coffin at my own Irish wake.

January third and the pounds multiplied; if this keeps up my goose is fried.

January fourth and the decorations look tacky; if I don't take them down someone'll think I am wacky.

January fifth and I'm out walking the hills; my feet feel great but, of course, I'm on pills.

January sixth is the feast for kings; I'm waiting for gifts of gold, frankincense and rings.

January seventh and I'm getting weary; eating only greens is making me teary.

January eighth and nothing seems to fit; I've been through all my closets and they've yielded not a whit.

January ninth is coming up; I told my husband to give me nothing for sup.

January tenth is almost done; as I look at the scale I know it's won.

January eleventh is very long, but I lost a pound and burst into song.

January twelfth, a day to remember, though I really wish it were already September.

January thirteenth might be unlucky this year; especially if I don't drink some beer.

January fourteenth is a nice round number; the days are short so I can enjoy my slumber.

January fifteenth and we're half-way through; I keep jogging but the pounds stick like glue.

January sixteenth and I'm starting the home stretch; if I lose a ton, my bikini I'll fetch.

January seventeenth and I long for spring; if I don't lose more weight my buttons will zing.

January eighteenth and all is well; the diet is working and life is swell.

January nineteenth and Chinese food last night; too much Kung Pao and I don't feel so light.

January twentieth and no one to blame; why do cookies keep calling my name?

January twenty-first, MLK is honored now; I wish I'd lost weight but I guess I don't know how.

January twenty-second and still no flowers; spring is coming and I'm counting the hours.

January twenty-third and I stop to wonder—can I lose ten pounds without another blunder?

January twenty-fourth is finally upon us; a few less inches and I'll fit on the bus.

January twenty-fifth looms on the horizon; if I try any harder I'll need a new lung.

January twenty-sixth and all through the day I'll be trying on clothes to give some away.

January twenty-seventh is finally near; soon I'll visit the doctor with nothing to fear.

January twenty-eight and I'm almost to the end; my choices for food must become my friend.

January twenty-ninth scurries in fast; a time to reflect on poor choices of the past.

January thirtieth and it's almost over; I might need a walking companion by the name of Rover.

January thirty-first and the month is finished; I should peek at the scale to see if I've diminished.

So there's a month of good and bad; I hope it went well or I'll be sad.

Thirty one days is all there is; I need to go to Oz and talk with The Wiz.

There's no more to say, I've run out of lines; it's not easy keeping up with these rhymes.

SEASONAL CELEBRATIONS

(How much is this going to cost us?)

How to Host a
New Year's Eve Party

It's crucial to plan a month in advance for an event as important as a New Year's Eve party. Make a list, check it twice, and try to recall who was naughty or nice... to you. Did someone bring you banana bread fresh out of the oven? Invite them. Did a friend loan you ten bucks when you forgot your wallet? Onto the list. That so-in-so who barrels past your house going 60? Cross him off the list and buy a box of tacks.

What to serve? You must offer mega multiples of every *hors d'ouevre* just in case people take more than the usual one or two. Don't forget you have to satisfy a lot of palates, diseases, and ailments. Becky's gluten intolerant, Bobby's diabetic, Bernie is a vegetarian and Barbie is vegan (confused yet?), Billy loves spicy and Bonnie (yes, ME) can't stand anything spicier than catsup. Don't forget Barry can't have salt.

Equal to food preparation is cleaning the house. When to start the tidying? Well, that is completely dependent on whether you have a cat or a dog. When we had a dog, I could do a lot of early preparation because the dog never jumped up on the dining room table and slept on the dinner plates. Owners of dogs have discovered that having a dog around is advantageous because dogs will slurp the crumbs and crumbles up as fast as they fall. Also, a dog is perfectly content to be put in the basement during the party and will be found fast asleep on his favorite chair. Cats, on the other hand, have to check out everything you are doing. As you are cleaning the toilet, they are dipping their paws in the water, leaping down and padding across your nice waxed floor leaving lovely little paw prints. Putting the cat in the utility room during the party is tantamount to animal abuse according to the covenant you signed with your cat when he allowed himself to be adopted by you.

If you are a cat owner, you wait till the last minute to start any party projects because you know your cat will give you the cold shoulder for weeks if you put him in the back room too early.

What to wear to your own soiree? You assume everyone will come in their New Year's Eve finest, but that won't happen. It will be jeans to suits to pajama bottoms with a sprinkling of sparkly, silvery, dangly, and spangly. Furs, fingernails, and fake eyelashes will be brought out for the occasion—hopefully attached to all the correct places. The host needs to be comfortable, to look like you are dressed to the teeth without making any of your guests feel that they are not. I recommend diamond earrings with Birkenstocks.

Arranging the room is important. If your friends are somewhat decrepit then they need to sit. But, sitting can lead to sleepiness. Sleepiness leads to snoring. Snoring isn't great accompaniment to background music. Then the spouse of the snorer gets mad and drags the offending mate home. That usually starts a mass exodus. To counteract this, you need bright lights, loud music, and games. Yes, games! Board games, card games, and the best game of all—a version of musical chairs where each time someone gets up to have another bite from the buffet, you sneak over and move their chair to another part of the room.

If your friends are my age, then it will be a challenge to get them to stay till midnight. Trick them by having the TV set to Hawaii. Or, have several TV sets on and let them choose the midnight they are most comfortable celebrating. And don't forget, you might need to provide some alternate transportation for those that have a glass or two of something stronger than eggnog. Let them know that you have a vehicle (your cousin's rusted-out flatbed truck) waiting. The next day they'll tell their friends what a good time they had in the one-horse open sleigh.

Oh, are you looking for an invitation from us? When that big ball drops we'll be fast asleep, visions of good investments dancing in our heads, cats nestled all snug in their beds. What, you thought *we* were going to have a party? Are you nuts? We can't stay up that late!

Christmas Greetings to All

It's the end of the year, 2014 will close,
I'm sorry as heck to see it all *goes*,
I feel old and worn out and lost as all hell,
I probably need to sit down for a spell.
Should I really tell you all that went on?
It was boring as gravy and not that much fun.
We did sell our boat, which was very good news
I went straight to the mall and bought 8 pairs of shoes.
Jim traded down for a new fishing boat,
I stay on the patio where I don't have to float.
Jim had some surgery, bladder 'bout burst,
Darn getting old when the prostate gets *worst*.
No surgeries for me, no weddings to plan
I'm still writing my mystery about killing poor Stan.
We kept up with friends, played cards all the time,
We don't play for money so we spent not a dime.
My Mah Jongg cohorts are as committed as I
We laugh and we talk and sometimes eat pie.
I'm busy with meetings about writing and crime

Bonnie Willemssen

I'm learning a lot about toeing the line.
We went to Florida to visit some friends
And drank so much OJ we needed Depends.
Stringing buttons on bracelets is my latest hobby
I made so darn many I might need a *jobby*.
I now speak at events and sell my new books
I rely on my talent, instead of my looks.
I did a sleep study—that was a blast,
I flunked the test and now wear a mask.
I found a nutritionist by the name of Diane,
Like the *little engine*, she makes me believe *I can*.
Ann is great; she has a new job,
She works from home where there isn't a mob.
Her firm is consulting, it's called UPD,
She helps city governments, but it's all Greek to me.
Erik, her spouse, in the Senate he works
In the Capitol Dome is where he asserts.
He watches the money for the appropriations committee
And also he's smart and terribly witty.
So, there it is, our year in review
Thank you so much for letting me spew.
We wish you good days in the upcoming year
If we don't hear from you we'll both shed a tear
So, send us your greeting and say your hello
Did you win the lottery and are rolling in dough?
A Happy New Year, may the future be all bright,
bonniewillemssen@gmail.com is our email, so please y'all write.

Step on a Crack, Break Your Mother's Back

Beware the Ides of March! It was my mother's obsession—the Ides of March. Why? No clue, but I had it marked on my calendar for years as if it were a birthday memo or anniversary reminder. Then one year, while I was transferring information from one date book to another I realized that I didn't care much about the Ides of March anymore. I had bigger things to occupy my attention: global warming, world famine, muggers, and swimsuit season. But, despite the demotion of March 15th (bad for Julius Caesar but good for me as I love Caesar salads), I still had to contend with all the Friday the 13ths that continually show up no matter how unwanted. And here comes another one this month. Lordy! How is a gal to survive such a day? And can you believe this? Somehow I ended up being the parent of not one, but two black cats? They were wonderful so I decided *that* omen was definitely debunked, but there are still ladders and broken mirrors and spilled salt to contend with. Friday the 13th is not to be taken lightly, you know. And if you are reading this, you probably realize that I survived, none the worse for wear, the two Friday the 13ths in 2012 so far. Don't get too excited yet because there is one more hurdle to overcome—*July* 13th.

I'm going to share some important facts about Friday the 13th with you, so pay attention: hope you do not hear anything new *this* Friday because apparently it adds another wrinkle to your face and a year to your age. I swear. Wikipedia says it's so. And, please, no matter what, don't sit at a table with 12 other people and, if you do, make sure you all sit down at exactly the same minute or the last one to sit down will be toast (not the same as *toasted*) before the year is over. A table for 13, are they kidding? I can barely get dinner ready for my husband and myself, much less 11 other people. The only danger of anyone dying after sitting at my dinner table is food poisoning—and I've never poisoned anyone... lately.

Actually, most people are especially careful on Friday the 13th, so statistically, fewer accidents happen on that day. I guess we are all tiptoeing on eggshells, or possibly the 21 million people in the United States who live in fear of that day are just staying out of vehicles and off bridges and not walking under ladders.

Because this is leap year, we have had to endure three Friday the 13ths, but next year, whoopee ding, there are only going to be two, and in 2014, hallelujah, only one. Just so you know, any month that begins on a Sunday will have a Friday the 13th in it, so, if you really want to keep bad luck from finding you, just change all the months on your calendars that begin on a Sunday to begin on a Saturday instead. Or mix it up a bit and have them begin on a Monday. Of course, there might be a titch of a problem with that because by day two you will be out of step with the rest of the world, but, oh well, no Friday the 13th for you.

By the way, I read that Julia Child died on Friday the 13th (in 2004). The lesson to be learned from this is that you should never, ever cook on any Friday the 13th, or any Friday, or any day with 13 in it, or multiples of 13, or with a 1 or 3, or a 31. I won't be taking any chances, that's for sure. Caution is my middle name. Another thing to be wary of are people with 13 letters in their names. Can you say Charles Manson, Jeffrey Dahmer, and Theodore Bundy? If something strange happens to me, be sure to question my faithful husband and my loving daughter— who both have 13 letters in their names. I think people with 13 letters in their name should start a club, not dissimilar to the Red Hat Club. They could call it the *Paraskevidekatriaphobia Club*. Membership includes staying in bed all day on Friday the 13th, covers over your head, waiting till midnight for the mother of all bad-luck days to end. Membership in the club is $13 but no one ever pays and the annual meeting is always on Friday the 13th so no one ever attends.

Be glad you are not living in ancient Rome. I know it would have been cool to see the Coliseum while they were building it, lions and all, and order pizza from the pagan venders outside of the Pantheon, but, Fridays were *execution* days during that era. It gives new meaning to TGIF, doesn't it?

I leave you with this warning: never change your sheets on a Friday; it will bring you bad dreams. Well, at last, a good explanation for those dreams where you are running to your classroom and just as you burst through the door, you look down and notice you are in your tighty-whities, and they're not even your best ones.

Hopefully all these facts have armed you for action—or inaction—whichever you choose. I will leave you with this last suggestion: Keep a salt shaker handy, put a rabbit's foot on your keychain, find a 4-leaf clover and, if all else fails, KEEP YOUR FINGERS CROSSED!

Rockin' Around The Christmas Tree In My Wooden Rocking Chair

Time has a way of speeding up as you get older. Notice I said as YOU get older. Jim and I are not aging. No, we are spry as elves jazzed up on candy cane coleslaw, stewed gingerbread fudge and eggnog omelets. So, what the heck happened? How did Christmas creep up on me? I knew it was coming *sometime* in the future, but how could twelve months have passed since last we did the Jingle Bell Rock? I vaguely remember buying Halloween candy last July and seeing shelves of wrapping paper and twinkly lights, but I thought it was leftovers from Christmas 2012. I guess it was just Yule-mart trying a new marketing strategy....the early reindeer gets the worm.

I did finish getting our house decorated for Christmas. You can come rest with the other merry gentlemen that have brought gifts of golf, frankfurters, and mirth. One of the three wise guys told us it was politically correct to use the words *Happy Holidays* in polite company, especially in December, so for years I did just that. My mother was adamant that I not write Christmas as "Xmas" when I was young or You Know Who would run you over with his sleigh. Now, if I use it when I'm in a hurry, I feel the dagger eyes of my mom boring into me and I can almost feel the stinging slap on my knuckles from Sister Mary R-E-S-P-E-C-T.

In early December I was cleaning out the Christmas closet (yes, I said Christmas, so sue me!) and what to my wondering eyes appeared but a miniature rolling pin and eight tiny cookie cutters. Just in time for family traditions. Last year I stuffed all the left over decorations onto the shelves, slammed the door, and held my breath as I tiptoed away. And it came to pass that a star appeared in the heavens and it was time to open the closet. Actually that's not what happened. What really occurred was some horrible, nasty, dirty SNOW fouled up everything. It's a four-letter word, you know—SNOW. I am petitioning for a Midwest motto to be adopted by January 1st: SAY NO TO SNOW! I want snow police, specially trained, to zap those fuzzy flakes before they accumulate on the ground. You always wanted a white Christmas? Rent the movie! Would you rather slip and slide in your one horse open sleigh or wouldn't it be *snow* much nicer to roast chestnuts by an open fire on a beach somewhere, with hula girls and cabana boys to remind you that the weather outside is *not* frightful? *Mele Kalikimaka* is the thing to say on a bright, Hawaiian Christmas Day. I'm dreaming of a green Christmas, just like the ones I…well, I never knew any green Christmases when I was young. But, that's my Christmas wish for next year—a Christmas of a different color.

Did you go shopping at the last minute this year? Or did you plan ahead and have everything for Bertha and Zoe and Elijah and Olivia by Nov. 1st? In case you forgot, I have OCD so my shopping was finished by the Ides of March.

I guess there was some excitement on Christmas Eve. Did you hear what I heard? Up on the rooftop? Hark, it was the angels singing, accompanied by the little drummer boy. All the faithful went wassailing and there was joy in the world. Unfortunately, Grandma got run over by a reindeer but it was right after she caught Mommy kissing Santa Claus, so run, Rudolph, run, 'cause jolly old St. Nick is coming down the chimney and when he sees you he's going to put his finger aside of his nose and advise you to go tell it on the mountain. Grandma only wants her two front teeth for Christmas, but she added some of her favorite things to the list so, Santa Baby, you need to take that sleigh for a ride so everyone can have a holly, jolly Christmas.

As for us, we were home for Christmas, having a silent night, nestled in our bed, asleep. But, then I sprang from my bed to see what was the matter when I heard the bells on Christmas morn. Hope you had yourselves a merry little Christmas and rocked around the Christmas tree in your wooden rocking chair.

NOTE: I don't ever give credence to commercial products, but I have to tell you that if you are inclined, you can buy an edible nativity set made of chocolate. Yes, that's right, chocolate. I swear. I saw it in Good Housekeeping. So, if you are sitting around the tree on Christmas Eve and someone gets hungry, you can direct them to the nativity set and invite them to gobble up Joseph or an angel or maybe baby Jesus. I'm just going to leave you to ponder that scenario.

Who Gets to Take Home the Ring?

I have been waiting all season for Super Bowl Sunday. I can't believe it's finally here. Counting down the days has been more exhilarating than an Advent Calendar with chocolate treats behind each door. Friends, invited to share in the excitement, have been on pins and needles for weeks. Like being in the locker room before the game, my heart is starting to thump, thump, thump.

I have my lucky shirt and socks which I wear each year in anticipation of that starter whistle blowing. How can I ensure a favorable outcome if I don't adhere to traditions? I've discussed with my husband the ground rules. There will be no weeping and gnashing of teeth – there will be no chest bumping in the TV room—there will be no pouring of Gatorade before, during or after the game. The dining room looks like a mock tailgate party....chips, dips, beer and soda served in and on cheap plastic and naturally no forks, knives or spoons are required.

And just as the first guys ring our doorbell, I pull a quarterback sneak and jump in my car to collect their wives as we head out for the Tucson Gem and Mineral Show. Surely you didn't think I was going to stay and watch something only slightly less boring than cleaning the moldy grout around my toilet? I think not! I told you I've been eagerly awaiting this day. Jim never notices I'm gone 'cause he's so preoccupied with his exciting (read: dumb) football game.

Going to the gem show is actually not unlike the Super Bowl– we wait at the gate till the kickoff – well, it's really just the doors opening but the anticipation is the same. There is a stampede of broad-shouldered women hustling to make the best moves on the playing field that they can. All are armed with large catch-all bags for their purchases and the smart ones bring water so the bright lights don't dehydrate them. Tripping and falling at the gem show might be certain death when people tackle each other in their push to the tables. Talk about unnecessary roughness!

My girlfriends and I have formed a Fantasy *Gem Show* League. Each member of the team has to show they found the deepest discounts and the best bargains. If someone gets a piece of Russian alexandrite at *cost* it's worth six points, an African Iolite would be one extra point if the seller puts it in a *unique* box and Chinese cloisonné is three points but only if the buyer pays *cash*. We revel in our status as football widows as we are dazzled by the glitz before us. There isn't a booth or vendor that doesn't benefit from our burning desire for trinkets and they happily accept the three C's – cash, checks and credit cards – oops, that's *four* C's isn't it?

If I take friends that have never been to the gem show before, I conduct an introductory class. It covers proper footwear, where the port-a-potties are located, what to do about the hot, bright lights that are intended to make the gems sparkle while you feel you're going through the *change*—again! Parking, lunch breaks and which tents have the best bargains is gladly passed on to my adoring students who look up to me—the Queen of All Things Glitter. And know this—Tucson weather is not as predictable as the Chamber of Commerce likes you to believe. I've experienced rain, snow, freezing temps and 90 degree days in February – sometimes all on the same day.

Often the day goes into overtime. We've run up and down the field multiple times. We know we've scored touchdowns but are still slightly short of winning that Lombardi Trophy and we must make one last blitz to ensure our victory. There cannot be any illegal substitutions – we have to make the goal by ourselves. It won't be long before we can pat each other's behinds and run home for a shower. The best part of the gem show, unlike the Super Bowl, is that you can do it all over the next day – and every day for the next two weeks.

At the end of the day cheers and high fives accompany our travels home to safety. The winning team has been determined and been awarded their rings. We all did the end zone dance and now we huddle in the car for the ride home.

Ghosts and Goblins and Ghouls, Oh My!

I t's Halloween again? Yippee! I mean, it's all about the candy, right? In our house my husband chooses the bags of treats. That's because he picks sweets he likes to have leftover. He also counts out each piece so we know exactly how many little "monsters" come to the door. He's very organized (read: obsessive). Last year we had nine, I think. Still, we buy enough candy to feed an army should an army happen to come by on All Hallows Eve. My mom got so few trick-or-treaters in her neighborhood that she started to give out dollars. I bet some kids circled around and came back for more—a dollar back in 1988 wasn't too bad. Come to think of it, that's pretty good even today.

I know none of you have done this in your household, but in ours we buy the treats early 'cause, you know, there might be a shortage closer to the actual event. Then we hide our stash (out of sight, out of mind) and come Oct. 28 we search high and low and when we finally find it… oh, oh, we discover that thieves have obviously snuck in and stolen all but five pieces of our hoard. Of course, neither Jim nor I would pilfer our own candy, but we decline to call the local sheriff. Luckily, when we march back to the store they still have candy. Go figure.

When we lived in La Crosse, Wisconsin, vans would park at the end of our circle and off-load dozens of little urchins to race around to each house as fast as they possibly could, collecting loot in big pillow cases. Now-a-days parents can just program the 'best' neighborhood (tweeted from kid to kid) into their GPS systems. So, you never know how many you'll actually have from year to year.

When I was young, my costume was a sheet or maybe some of mom's costume jewelry or better yet, a broom with an old black skirt. Nothing was elaborate. My goal was to wear something that allowed me to remove my glasses ('cause they fogged up) each time I went into a house for a treat. Yes, in the old days we were welcomed in; now we throw the candy at their retreating bodies as they scurry to the next yard. Luckily we don't have to worry about running over little ones in the street because all costumes come with enough LED lights to look like a float in the Torchlight Parade during the La Crosse Oktoberfest.

Sigh! No invites to a costume party this year. Probably best when I remember the year that we went to our lawyer's house for a party and Jim wore a prisoner costume with a printed sign saying "JOHN DOE (substitute real name here) WAS MY LAWYER." Once, I borrowed a long, brown wig for my gypsy costume and a gal I met at the party said, "Well, at least I'll know you if we meet in the grocery store." I laughed and had to confess that I was wearing a wig and was really a short-haired blond.

I assure you that I happily make as much fuss over this sacrosanct day of "feasting" as I do over Easter, Thanksgiving, and Christmas. I have ghost sweatshirts, pumpkin earrings, blinking witch broaches, and of course, rings and bracelets, watches and scarves to match all my Halloween clothing. However, this year I've decided to just be myself—a frumpy, crotchety, rundown, tired out old lady. I won't even need to buy any special makeup; sallow skin and gray hair don't cost a cent. And because I had my knee replacement only a couple of weeks ago, my walker will complement the ensemble perfectly.

Actually, I know my husband is going to be keeping a close watch on me for Halloween because I'm taking all these lovely pain killers. I kind of think they are better than candy, but eventually I'll have to wean myself off of them. I imagine if I went out to trick-or-treat this year, people would be giving me Metamucil, denture cream, and cans of Ensure. The joys of getting older! Jim told me he wants me to answer the doorbell when it rings tonight 'cause he's sure the children will be tossing their candy at ME, either out of fear or sympathy. Trick or treat.

Wherefore Art Thou Spring?

I know that's not an exact quote from Shakespeare, but I think I'm safe; he's dead and he can't sue me. So did any of you notice we had the first day of spring already? Spring manifested herself on March 20th. Did you miss it? I'm pretty sure some special things were supposed to happen right after that day, like crocus sprouting, maybe some trees budding or at the very least some birds chirping their welcome to warmer days. Ha! Spring apparently does not concur. Isn't it her job to coordinate and cooperate with the laws of nature? Or maybe Spring is getting older, like the rest of us, and is confused as to her role and can't recollect what activities should happen when. Of course, I should be sensitive to those of you who probably do not look forward to spring. Those who suffer from the allergies that tree and grass pollen deliver may have bribed Spring to come later in hopes of avoiding the Season of Sneezin.' Don't forget snakes and black bears hibernating in their rocky bedrooms are probably happy to continue their long winter's nap. No one, not animal, mineral or vegetable, wants to wake up when it's chilly if they can stay snuggled in their warm down-filled blankets.

 You know why I like spring—the *first* day of spring? Because there are only two days a year when there are 12 hours of light and 12 hours of dark and as a person with OCD I thrive on the symmetrical. Plus, I also love lilacs, so if there is a hint of lilac buds under the lingering four feet of snow, I'm thrilled.

Not everyone goes by the calendar to embrace spring. When I was young, storm window removal was the official opening of spring in our household. My dad pulled the storm windows off when there was no chance of any more cold – usually around June 1st. That was a long time to wait to open our windows. My husband was not quite as excited for the familial event that ushered in spring in his household because his dad made him paint the house every summer – idle hands are the devil's something or other.

People are always meeting in the grocery store or at the yoga studio or at the race track and exchanging little tidbits of intel on recent sightings that are absolutely positively definitely without a doubt a sign that spring has sprung. Those darn squirrels are an encouraging sign that spring is upon us. Such cute little things, slipping across ice and snow, checking their tiny GPS' to find last year's nuts. Bluebirds are the hardiest of birds and usually first to arrive in the spring. I think scientists discovered that their feathers are blue from genetic selection…or something Darwiny like that. But, I know the real reason they call them bluebirds—they are *blue* from the freezing weather because they always try to beat all the other birds back to the Midwest. And we cannot forget those daffy ducks that fly back every spring in V formation. Apparently, the "V" has been handed down from generation to generation as the most efficient way to fly. *Question*: Do you know why one side of the V is longer than the other? Answer: Because there is one extra bird on that side. Ha Ha! Did you get it?

So, yippee! Snow seems to be dwindling. Icicles are dripping their little tails off, and snow plow drivers are sooooo ready to hang it up for the next two seasons. The pots of geraniums you stored in your basement over the winter are leafing. The Kentucky Derby is already listed in your TV Guide. Whoopee, a chance to wear big outrageous hats and suck down mint juleps at an alarmingly acceptable rate—if you wanted to look stupid in a hat or waste your calories on a green drink. I think I need to find a different "starting point" for MY spring. Next year I'm just going to throw a dart at the calendar and declare that day BONNIE'S

OFFICIAL SPRING DAY.

Mark Twain said: "In the spring, I have counted 135 different kinds of weather inside of twenty-four hours." If he were standing in front of me today I'd say, "Are you crazy? You must have channeled Rip Van Winkle on the day you counted 'cause there are soooooo many more than just 135." I'm almost positive. Don't you agree Minnesota and Wisconsin and Michigan and Iowa and North/South Dakota and Canada? And last but not least, I cannot close without trash talking that little rodent in Punxsutawney, Pennsylvania. We are now nine weeks out from February 2nd and it no longer matters whether he saw his shadow or not – he had six weeks – good or bad – and he blew it.

Deck the Halls With Balled-Up Holly

I'm the queen of decorations. Any holiday, any excuse. I've been known to decorate for April Fools' Day, Groundhog Day, Sugar Cane Day (think cookies), the day that commemorates the invention of the VCR, and do you think something as important as Tear Off Those Pillow Tags Day would go unnoticed in my house? No way. But when it comes to the big three—Halloween, Thanksgiving, and Christmas—I'm like a mad scientist. I can mix, match, mingle, jumble, tangle and combine something to fit every nook and cranny of our house. No surface is off limits. Mirrors, doors, shelves, shoes, mouthwash bottle, the toilet lid, and who doesn't love a little surprise when you open the freezer and up pops a snowman? Some might say I overdo the decorations a tad. My daughter and husband come to mind, but I say if a little bit's good, a lot must be better. Right? Never mind, this is my story and I can't hear you anyway.

I came by this obsession with decorating naturally. My mother loved all holidays, too. However, she insisted on a religious theme for all her decorations. Case in point: She loved May Day because she could set out her statue of the Virgin Mary with vases of fresh flowers. Mary's tiny crown was checked each day to make sure it was still straight. Sometimes I would walk home from school and find my mother kneeling in front of the altar she had erected for the duration of the month. I am pretty sure she watched out the window for me to start up the block after school and then counted to 20 and knelt down just moments before I walked in the door. She would then sigh, struggle to get herself up from that position she had held for all of 60 seconds, and tell me she hoped I had had a good day in school 'cause she was praying for me to get a good grade on my spelling test. I would then feel so guilty that I had only gotten 8 out of 10 correct. After all, my poor mother had prostrated herself in supplication for me.

Flash forward. I am not religiously oriented like my dear ol' mum. My decorations for various times of the year run the gamut of big red hearts and cupids on Valentine's Day, a four-foot leprechaun on the door on St. Patrick's day, bunnies, chicks and tulips at Easter, turkeys, pilgrims and pumpkins at Thanksgiving, and Santa, sleighs and elves at Christmas. I really did (notice the past tense) decorate for every occasion listed on the calendar. It's why I became an elementary school teacher. Not only could I decorate my house every way from Sunday if I wanted (note: I'm speaking of my house, not my mother's cathedral), but I could decorate my classroom for each new month and each new holiday. I was in seventh heaven.

You should have seen the storage room in our old house. Carefully labeled boxes and boxes and boxes, stacked one on top of the other, waiting silently until pressed into service. When I still had energy, before I got old and grumpy and tired, I used to decorate two trees; the formal living room tree and the informal fun tree in the family room. What was I thinking? I can remember the year my mom said she was not going to put up a tree. I just about had a conniption fit! It was the end of the world as I knew it. The apocalypse, the End of Days. It was 12/21/12 on the Mayan calendar. So, I took over the job (joy) of decorating it for her, and when my daughter was old enough, she took over from me. Even in her nursing home I had a tree for my mom's room and decorated the bulletin board outside her room for years so all the residents would enjoy the changing seasons and upcoming holidays. You might call me a bit of a fussbudget, or worse, you might call me a (fill in the blank) but, you know that wherever I am, the house/hall/room will be festive, doggone it!

I would be remiss not to mention that I have a friend who decorates a tree in every room, and each room has a different theme. One is for golf, one is antique and family heirloom ornaments, one has all beanie babies on it, one is covered in every manner of penguins, and to tell you the truth, since she decorates seven trees, I can't really remember the other themes. And Christmas is just her secondary holiday. Halloween is her big event. Even I, the diva of decorations, the oracle of ornaments, the guru of garnish—even I am struck dumb (no comments about dumbness please) by the amount of witches, ghosts, goblins and spider webs lurking about her abode. To her, I tip my hat. But, next to her is my mom, and then me, me and me.

My daughter says things like, "I don't want any of that old stuff you keep bringing out, Mom." My husband says, "What, we're going to put up a tree again? That's so much work." Like I don't know how much work it is to put up all the decorations without help or applause. But, I do it. It's my tradition. It's my connection to my past. It's my reality. It's my… wait a minute, this is crazy. This year I'm going to leave all the decorations in the boxes and go on a cruise. Let someone else do the work. I'm just kidding. That'll never happen.

HODGEPODGE

(Why is the early bird special so late in the day?)

Diary of a Bad Housewife

Dear Diary: I woke up at 8 o'clock with the sun shining on my nightstand. I saw my husband had written "See you at noon" in the dust that caked the top of our dresser. We're a *green* family; no trees were destroyed in the conveyance of that message.

Dear Diary: When I got up at 8:15 this morning I realized I forgot to do laundry. No underwear! I made the laundry room my first priority. I don't mind washing clothes 'cause I can rest between trips to the washer/dryer by catching up on my soaps. Get it—me cleaning my *clothes* while watching *soaps*?

Dear Diary: I guess yesterday got away from me. I awakened at 8:30 today and realized we needed food for dinner. Now it's 5 o'clock and I find I need to be creative with leftover lima beans, soggy noodles, expired mushroom soup, and freezer-burned pork chops. I'll hold my breath while Jim eats, hoping my concoction won't kill him.

Dear Diary: Jim's stomach bothered him all night. No clue why. But, I sprang out of bed at 8:45 refreshed and ready to face the world. Well, face my household chores, anyway. Foremost was vacuuming. Vacuuming isn't difficult, and I always adjust it to the lowest setting so its tracks look like I worked really hard. Jim got home earlier than I expected from his errands, so I had to kick the remaining dust bunnies under the chair. I hope I'll remember them next time I have the urge to clean—in a month or so.

Dear Diary: I am getting further behind and don't know why. When I rolled out of bed at 9:00 today I pondered what I could do to get the house spic and span without exerting too much effort. I hatched a perfect plan—bellows from the fireplace tools. I could just blow the dust off the furniture and counters. It worked pretty well, but the floor now looks like an old-fashioned meat market.

Dear Diary: I gazed in the mirror after dragging myself from bed at 9:15 and lamented that no one appreciates my domesticity. I wondered how the mirror could reflect wrinkles that I'm pretty sure are not there. Anyway, to continue, I learned everything at my mother's knee: Scrub the floors every day, clean the toilets every day, iron sheets and towels, and your husband's boxers and undershirts. So, that's what I did for the first few years of our marriage. Sorry Mom, no disrespect, but you were nuts.

Dear Diary: As I was rubbing the sleep from my eyes at 9:30 this morning, I decided to put an ad in the paper for someone who would like to barter their cleaning skills for my laundry skills. (Shh, don't tell them about my soap theory.) I should add that I'd even throw in some cursory ironing as long as I can do it in front of the TV.

Dear Diary: No one responded to my newspaper ad. Darn. Over this week I've gotten most of the housework done. Laundry is clean, sheets are changed. Why can't we sleep on sheets for two months, again? The clutter is gone. I worked like a banshee from the moment I stirred awake at 9:45. I left a note for my husband, on the yet again dusty dresser, not to open the closet door. Did he heed my warning? No! The closet rained shoes, wrapping paper, pillows, paper napkins, and warranties from 45 previously purchased appliances.

Dear Diary: I knew when I roused myself at 10:00 that I was going to be in trouble today. Somewhere along the silver road of marital bliss, I lost my craving to cook. I waited till the last minute, hoping Jim would offer his culinary skills. Unfortunately, he has none. Would he take me out? No way. Could he just eat whatever he finds in the fridge and declare me a superb cook? Nope. Do I phone for pizza? Of course. The delivery guys don't need GPS to get to our door.

Dear Diary: After coming to the conclusion that I've been getting up much too early I had a sudden revelation: it's *sunshine* and *daylight* that make my house look dirty. So, now I just get up at dusk. Unfortunately, I still have to come up with a plan that eliminates cooking from my exhausting daily routine.

And, if I am Elected

Last week I joined a popular weight loss organization and discovered that my favorite pastime, shopping, isn't considered an activity. What an outrage! It's not even recognized by the Olympic committee, and for Heaven's sake, isn't there a town somewhere that has a Shopping Hall of Fame? Because of this egregious oversight I am going to run for president. Yes, of the United States. I know it's a little late to get my name on the ballot, but please just write me in. Be sure to spell it correctly or they will throw it out. It's your goddess-given right to be a citizen who communicates her wants and needs. So, whether you are an "elephant", a "donkey", a "tea drinker", dependent on your "independence", or even if you are a man, get out and vote.

Actually, I'd like to change the voting process, too. Wouldn't it be great if the two candidates with the highest number of votes became co-presidents? The office of vice-president has never had much clout, so we can just do away with it. Since the co-presidents most certainly will be from different political parties, we will need a third person to help settle disputes and that should be a representative of John Q. Public—or Bonnie Q. Public…that's me. And I am throwing my hat (well, I hate hats, so I'm throwing my curling iron) into the ring. I will run on the

Tie-Breaker Platform. I could be the person who listens carefully to all the arguments presented by both the top-vote getter and by the second-to-top vote getter. I would weigh the situation, consider all the ways it would affect, well, me, of course. Here is a for-instance: I'm asked to settle a dispute about whether schools around the country should end at 2 p.m. Now, if my daughter was young I'd be voting to keep kids in school till 8 p.m., getting home just in time for jammies, tooth brushing, and a goodnight kiss. Because she's grown, however, I would just wave my magic wand (as official tie-breaker I would insist on a glittery wand to wave) and declare that kids throughout the country get jobs at 15 and start supporting their elders.

Also, who was the idiot that decided that all toilet paper rolls in public bathrooms have to be housed in those metal containers and then mounted on the wall at ankle height? I'll make all states change them immediately. There would be decibel controls on music in restaurants. Caller ID has to work all the time. All places of business need golf cart shuttles for older folks (me, for instance) so that we don't have to walk too far with our purchases. That would just be good customer service, right? All calendars have to start with Sunday; sometimes they start with Monday and that confuses me.

Before the ink on the inaugural papers is dry, I would be proposing the extermination of all magazines that feature thin, beautiful, young women. It would be for the sake of the self-image of young girls everywhere, of course, not because I look terrible in comparison. That would be shallow of me.

When my job as Bonnie Q. Public becomes a fixture in the minds of all Americans, I will set up a website for suggestions, replacing the suggestion box left over from the Roosevelt administration. Each and every one of you who vote for me will be allowed to make suggestions at the site. I have far reaching powers (don't forget my magic wand), and I will know if you voted for me or not. Also, while in office, I intend to start Zumba lessons in the Lincoln Library every Wednesday; movies, popcorn and super-sized soda in the rotunda every Friday, and my favorite, a *Knit and Hurl* group every Tuesday for gossip in the Oval Office, but, only when Prez One and Prez Other One are off kissing babies, appearing on Saturday Night Live, and doing stuff like, oh, running the nation.

I am confident that you will see the simplicity of my ideas. Money for babies and puppies and kittens? Pass that without discussion. Money for war? No way, no how. Money for the moon? Over the top. Money for mooning? Not even being considered. Money for my five star resort extravaganza? Approved!

My platform? Well, it's simple. BONNIE, BONNIE, SHE'S THE ONE. VOTE FOR HER FOR NUMBER THREE. You expected poetry?

Raining Cats and Dogs

Do you have a pet? Kitty, puppy, guppy, turtle, bunny or snail? They say that owning a pet, especially one that you can actually PET, lowers blood pressure and creates a sense of well-being. Really? So when the cat leaves lovely hair balls on the couch and further justifies his existence by dropping a mouse at your feet, does that lower my blood pressure? When the dog refuses to leave her "gift" in the empty lot, but will gladly grace the manicured lawn of the persnickety neighbor, is that giving me a sense of well-being? I think not! And don't get me started on the fish in the fishbowl. You know, the pretty colored ones that blow kisses at you on day one, hide from you on day two, and on day three they're tummy up in the tank. My daughter named her first two fish *Lunch* and *Dinner*. Perhaps more life sustaining names would have helped.

I tried my luck with a pond once, buying the round molded form complete with the fountain. I bought filters, lilies, fish food, and carp, all to enhance quiet contemplation. The next morning, two of my fish were missing. What the heck? Did they run away? Not likely since they don't have feet. Unsolved mystery. A day later my husband, Jim, wakes me to announce that the expensive plants I had in the pond were gone.

Slight traces of them led into the bushes. Not being dummies, we both concluded, "Raccoons!" Next day a friend visited. She laughed as she looked at the pyramid of lawn chairs I had perched over the pond to keep out those black-eyed hooligans. Unfortunately, the chairs only delayed them, and next morning all the fish were gone. By afternoon the pond was cleaned and returned to the store.

Ever have a bird? Ann named ours Tweet-Tweet. They were studying onomatopoeia in school. Only problem, birds give me the creeps. But, I was trying to enrich my kid's life…after all, she might have been a budding veterinarian. Apparently she was born with the "birds are yucky" gene also, because after a couple months she didn't want the bird either. We gave it away—lock, stock and cage.

Our golden retriever was a loving member of our household. After Taffy had gone to doggie heaven, Ann asked for a kitten. *Oh goodie*, thought her mother (that's me) a *kitten*? What do I know about kittens? But, on her 13th birthday we brought home a kitten. She named him Caesar Augustus, as they were studying Ancient Rome in school. A year later another feline friend, Leo the Lion (they were either studying astrology or zoology), joined our family. He was the Yin to Augie's Yang. They completed each other. Augie happily taught Leo to jump up on the kitchen counters. Leo gleefully taught Augie to jump on the back of a chair and push it over. They both thought it was a giggle and a half to jump up and turn off light switches. Gradually I went from dog lover to cat lover.

I've had a snake (who fooled me and crawled out of the box) and turtles (the last one snapped my finger and ended up at Myrick Park monkey pond), and when I was young, a dachshund, who waddled along on her little legs till she was tired, at which point she would give up and lie down in the street. She also had begging for table scraps down to a science once she realized what a pushover my father was. They would sneak ice cream in the dark kitchen every night as if my mother didn't know. A spoonful for dad, a spoonful for Heidi.

I really do love most animals. But, now, at a time when we want to travel and not have to worry about things at home, we are happily pet-free. (I have to stop writing now, tears are corroding my computer as I think of all the pets I've loved and lost.) I guess I should say Jim and I are satisfied with the mobility of no pets. Well, that's not it exactly; it's more of recognition that it's convenient to have no pets. Well, darn it, I hate not having a pet. I need to find the pet that would require the least amount of work. One that can fetch my slippers and paper; one that can watch me with adoring eyes and greet me with excitement when I get home from shopping. Wait, I already have one! Jim!

Retail Therapy

There was always one job that I really wanted to apply for in my hometown. It was called "secret shopper" and it meant that the store hired you to shop and then report to the home office on the salesperson's behavior. How a sales person behaves was not really a big concern of mine, but being paid to shop—now that would be a dream come true, but I never saw an ad for that position. Darn.

They say shopping is the act of buying things you don't need with money you don't have. Like I care. I will continue shopping for furniture, gewgaws, clothes, don't get me started on shoes, and jewelry, which is a bigger expense, but, oh what fun to sparkle till you farkle. I adore purse shopping. I think my love of purses started back in yesteryear when white shoes had to match the white purse, tan shoes/tan purse, and so on. I'm only following the advice passed on to me by my shopaholic mother. It's not my fault. I learned at her knee the joys of holding up a credit card and saying "Charge it, please."

Actually, shopping with her was like running a marathon—endless, tiring, and sweaty. Okay, Mother would never have sweat nor let me sweat, so strike that last one. We would put on sensible shoes (depending on my age it was saddle shoes when I was ten or one-inch heels when I was sixteen) and off we'd go to pound the pavement. She loved Minneapolis, and my dad would drive us to the Burlington station for the 4 A.M. train which, despite stopping at every burg along the route, would still get us to the Twin Cities before the stores opened. Our routine was to go to the Forum Cafeteria to eat breakfast. Then our day really began. Mother would march us in and out of every store on Nicollet Avenue.

When we needed a break, we headed to Dayton's. Placing our purchases in a locker, we would then ride up the escalator (I loved the escalator) to the 12th floor to eat in either the bright and sunny tea room or the dark but elegant Oak Room. With only a day to shop, we didn't linger over lunch and soon we were weaving our way around walkers, hawkers, and gawkers. Our dinner tradition was the Nanking Chinese Restaurant. Soon a taxi took us to the Milwaukee Road train station for the 7 p.m. departure.

My dad would be waiting for our arrival. Exhausted, I could barely keep my eyes open, but my mother, Shopper Extraordinaire, chatted to my dad about our adventures and our purchases. The next day she would try on her outfits for him. First the violet suit with the hip length jacket that sported three gold buttons and a matching pencil thin skirt with a four-inch slit up the back. Then she would model the red suit with the waist-length jacket that sported five silver buttons and a matching pleated skirt, and she'd ask my dad which one he liked. Dad was smart. His answer was always the same. "Take them both, Mary." So, when I got married, I tried to score two outfits from my new husband. His response would be, "For Pete's sake, you have too many clothes in the closet as it is. Can you take them back?" Darn. Where did this poor boy grow up?

For those of you that feel you might need some help with your shopping compulsion, I did some research. I belong to a group of people who meet secretly in basements of department stores all over the country to discuss their shopping addiction. For some, their downfall is the flash of the blue light special, others are tortured by the smell of new leather, and still others cannot walk past a 50 percent off sign in a store window. The lure is so great that they find themselves inside, gleefully grabbing items off the shelves. When this happens to me, and I come home with a trunk load of treasures, I reason with my husband that I purchased it all at 50 percent off, and he explains to me that I paid 50 percent more than I would have had I not bought it at all. Poor guy, he's so confused.

I have actually learned a lot at these SA (Shopper's Anonymous) meetings. I learned the benefits of taking old stuff to the resale shop so I get money and room in my closet for more purchases. I have practiced this form of closet purging faithfully. My husband says that I might as well take the new things right to the resale shop. What does he know? He must have thought I was attending those meeting to get *over* my shopping addiction. Get real!

Here are my suggestions for a twelve-step withdrawal program to help you become a non-shopper:

1. Glue car doors shut.
1. I can't think of any more.

If you need any help, call me and we'll go shopping. That's what a shopping sponsor is supposed to do, right?

Small Town Fever

Coming from the BIG city of La Crosse, Wisconsin I wasn't sure how I was going to handle living in the small town of Brownsville, Minnesota. When we moved here it held a café, a pizza place, several bars, a gas station/convenience store, a post office, a community center, two churches, and a volunteer fire department. Most of our needs were taken care of, except the church we wanted to attend only had services on Sunday morning at 8. Eight in the morning!!!! For a gal who rolls out of bed at 8:30 at the *earliest* that was not going to work for me. But, special things started happening in our new home town. We attended Brownsville Days and there was a cute parade with candy galore being thrown to the bystanders. My husband mowed many a two year old down getting to it, and by the following year those little tykes knew to watch the parade from the other side of the street cause that 'big guy' could run faster. (I'm kidding. Jim always shared his "loot" with the "other" kids around him.) We toured our volunteer fire department and were amazed at how up-to-date and well-stocked it was, not to mention all those cute firemen. We went on a rare tour of the local museum, lovingly renovated by caring people in the area. And I've read every word of Brownsville's history, written by several locals. Also, I found some of my relatives are from Brownsville.

We came to love our life in a town with a population of 517. We thought that it would go up by two when we moved in, but the postmistress was quick to quip that "Farmer Jones" had died, and so the sign could only be updated by one. This was when Jim began his daily walk to the post office to kid with Barb, who could dish it out as well as she could take it. The Copper Penny became a special place to walk to for lunch. Well, Jim and I would walk, but our friends (he's a retired dentist from Caledonia but I'm not naming any names) would drive the whole three blocks because his wife was afraid of seeing a snake. Which, come to think of it, was not as unlikely as one might think because we are below the bluffs and on the path where the snakes slither to get to the river.

As my circle of Brownsville friends grew, so did my interest in branching out to new towns in my new state of Minnesota. It took years for me to stop saying I was from Wisconsin. Now I say it correctly the first time so people don't think I'm an escapee from a mental ward when I say, "I'm from Wisconsin. Oh, wait, no I'm not. I moved. I meant to say I'm from Minnesota."

I've made the acquaintance of some wonderful Caledonia, Minnesota gals. One of them is my editor for this very paper (Diana) and the very one you can blame or bless for my monthly column. So, what did I discover in Caledonia besides good friends? I discovered some great restaurants and some fun gift shops, and people who know each other and each other's business—for better or worse. I've even discovered that people are not paranoid about their possessions and property like I was in La Crosse. I, the most OCD person you will ever encounter, am floored when I walk past someone's purse sitting on the chair while they run to the restroom at The Farmhouse, or I walk past the open windows of a car on a warm day, packages sitting on the passenger seat while shoppers enjoy The Pine Cone Place. Everyone greets you, all want to know how you are, most are interested enough to chat for a while, and a few even recognize that connecting with another person is the key to a happy life. And small town living is a happy life. Think of how clean everyone's lungs are (well, if they don't screw it up by smoking). And the stars? Aren't they wonderful on a clear night? When I drive between

Caledonia and Brownsville I marvel at the green pastures, with their wide rows of crops sweeping over and around the hills. In some places, houses or farms have paint peeling on their buildings, but the cows don't care.

There is a slow rhythm to a small town. The train whistle makes me think of traveling far and wide, but still coming back home to my small town existence. The Great River Road is well-traveled by many who seek a feeling of life in the slow lane, yet they whiz past at top speed, hurrying to the next site, forgetting to stop and "smell our dairy air." (That was once a suggestion for the new Wisconsin license plate.)

So, I'm glad we moved to Brownsville. I'm happy that I've made so many great friends. I'm thrilled that I can spend the rest of my life in a peaceful place without the rush and hubbub of traffic, long lines in the grocery store, and a Starbucks on every corner. Remember the TV show, Green Acres, from the late '60s? Oliver (played by Eddie Albert) and Lisa (played by Eva Gabor) leave their upscale condo in New York City for the rolling hills of Hooterville (no one snickered at that name back then). I was horrified that Oliver would force his wife to move to the country, complete with barns and farm animals and the quiet life. Now I know he had it right.

The Complete Idiot's Guide to Autos

Automobiles flummox me. I've tried to have a reasonable relationship with them. I've washed them when they're in my care, I've filled them with gas, I've opened my door carefully to avoid nicks, and I've made my husband check the tire pressure. So, once, when I called him because my vehicle stopped in the middle of the street, I didn't realize that I would need a really good excuse for why. You know, a story for the ages; *gorilla runs down road, flying saucer lands on lovers' lane, woman forgets to look at gas gauge!* My auto stopped because it had *no gas*. Empty. Dry. Nada.

Once, I "borrowed" my parents' Cadillac and drove it to the county fair (30 miles round trip). I planned on getting home before Mom and Dad had returned. But, I got busted! My parents got home early. Not having a license and never, ever having driven a car before was apparently a really bad thing according to my mother. My punishment was to not get my license for a year. What, no compliments on how great my novice driving skills were?

As a high school senior, I picked up a friend for choir practice. I had my dad's 1965 red Oldsmobile Cutlass and was excited to be out of "no-driving" purgatory. I was steering perfectly through the narrow pillars standing guard on each side of her driveway when one of them jumped out and scraped the side of my car. That's my story and I'm sticking with it! It seemed logical to me that I should continue to drive forward. In hindsight, that was definitely not the wisest choice, because when the scraping noises ceased, the passenger door wouldn't open. Shouldn't unusual occasions like this be taught in driver's education?

I might quickly tell you about a snow storm when I was driving over icy streets and a kid in front of me slammed on his brakes and I slid into his bumper. I guess they mean it when they talk about staying several car lengths behind. And, I could mention the time I discovered the meaning of the words "blind spot" when I slowly entered a divided highway where someone in my *blind spot* t-boned me. Is it my fault cars have design flaws?

I don't have trouble with just my own car; oh no, I'm an equal opportunity menace. The only dent in my daughter's car was when it was in our garage and I took a lawn chair off the wall and it fell on the hood. Till the day she sold it she reminded me of its pristine condition, except for *that* dent. By the way, my husband had a car stolen. Right out of the parking ramp while he was at work. Of course, everyone was like, "Oh, you poor guy, someone stole your car? How awful for you." What about me? I had to *share my* car with him for weeks.

Other people have trouble with their cars too, you know. A common activity when we grocery shop in our retirement community of Green Valley, Arizona is watching a grocery boy following a tiny couple up one row and down the other in the parking lot—his arm high, clicker in hand, hoping to hear the bleeping beep of the car, crying for its owners. I lost my car in a parking garage in Tucson once and had to have a patient police lady drive me up and around and down till I finally spotted my stupid car. I know you think *I'm* the stupid one, but I prefer to blame the car. What can it do? Cars can't talk. Yet.

One more anecdote. As many upsets as I have had with cars, at least I haven't been pulled over for reading while driving as my friend's mother was. Her explanation was she was late for a meeting and had to review her notes. She was ticketed and the notes were locked in the trunk—police orders.

Okay, this is the last story, I promise. When I was about ten, my mother drove over one of the concrete dividers in the grocery store parking lot. She was mortified and swore me to secrecy. The instant we got home I ran into the living room and tattled to my dad. I was a little snot back then. Now I'm a cool, calm, collected columnist and would never tattle—unless money was involved. Do feel free to bribe me.

The Great Outdoors

I am not thrilled with the way things are in the 21st century. You would think mankind would have found a way to enjoy the great outdoors without actually having to be *in* the great outdoors. Personally, I'm not a fan of communing with nature. Nature is full of birds and bees and acorns and trees, lions and tigers and bears. Mother Nature is a fickle lady, one minute flooding us out, next freezing our toes, then heaping on the white stuff—but those things I can handle. It's the bugs and flying insects and blowing germs and stuff that congregates outside that makes it impossible for me to enjoy *eating* outside. And can anyone tell me what is appealing about sitting in the sunshine on a patio only to have chilling clouds arrive minutes later? The reverse is also true. No sooner have you settled in a shady spot where you don't have to squint into the sun than the sun finds you faster than scientists have ever documented to enfold you in its fiery blaze. "Waiter, I need more ice in my tea!"

Is it fun to sit at a table where birds have recently been hopping around looking for crumbs and leaving little white drops? Any sane person wouldn't want to sit at a table near bushes and flowers that could harbor snakes or geckos or condors or hippos. Have you seen what an army of ants looks like when they're marching into the purse that you carelessly assumed would be safe at your feet? And obviously all manner of rodents could scamper across your shoes, or a bazillion bees might come buzzing by your bonnet.

My husband and I recently visited friends in Florida, the home of spiders, lizards, snakes and alligators. You see where I'm going with this, don't you? There must be something in the salt air from the Gulf that tricks people into thinking its soooooooo *special* to eat outside. What is so special, you might ask? I know I asked it—over and over and over again. Why in the name of all that is holy would a person knowingly and willingly and deliberately put themselves in danger? Mosquitoes carry West Nile disease, you know. Where have a fly's feet been before it lands on your fork or the lip of your glass? The layer of sand on the seat of your chair could have recently been beneath the dirty diaper of a toddler on the beach. Only one time did I acquiesce and grudgingly agreed to eat on the open porch of a restaurant. Can you guess what happened? A fly flew into my dressing and got stuck. As I stared in horror and disgust, calling on all the saints in Heaven to snatch me from my mortal coil, my husband grabbed my plate and got it out of my sight. A heroic effort, but too late! I would not eat another bite. Although, maybe I've invented a new diet plan: eat outside and lose your appetite. And what's next? Could one of the million pythons that have invaded Florida come slithering down the umbrella pole? Yes it could!

Anyway, after that horrific and distressing incident I would not agree to eat outside again. Two days later, we went to a classy restaurant and our hosts agreed we would eat inside to accommodate my OCD (Open-air Consumption Disorder). However, at the far end of the room, the whole wall opened to the deck. Believing that I was safe at the distance we were from that open wall, I was enjoying my meal when a bird flew in and dive-bombed our table. If these terrorist avian attacks can happen in the seemingly safe environs of the dining room, why would I ever agree to eat outside again?

My good friend Clare hates birds. Was it Alfred's influence? I don't know. All I know is that I can trust that whenever she and I are together we will never eat outside. It's such a relief. I have panic attacks worrying about being tricked into eating outside by some do-gooder who thinks if I try it I'll like it.

My conclusion is that outside is nice and all and fine for people who don't mind feasts with beasts, but, don't be offended if I run at breakneck speed over the river and through the woods to arrive safely inside the doorway of a restaurant with four solid walls and no patio.

Have I Got A Deal For You!

When I was young, there were only two big sales a year—the January white sales and the after the 4th of July clearance sales. You probably remember back when Halloween items were in the stores promptly on October 1st and Christmas didn't dare show its face till the day after Thanksgiving. In the town where I grew up, we waited with baited breath for the curtains on the picture window in the downtown department store to ceremoniously fall, revealing the delights beyond. It was such a thrill. The Christmas season was official on that day. As the years passed, sales became more popular, but back then, if my mom bought something on sale I had to keep it a secret. She didn't want her friends to know she hadn't paid full price—they would have thought she was cheap. Oh, times have changed! I wouldn't want my friends nowadays to know I paid full price for something. They would think I was a fool. But, I'm off track. I really want to discuss my obsession with getting a discount on everything I buy. I comb newspapers and the internet culling coupons for restaurants and stores. I only purchase items that match the coupons or are marked at least half off. I hate it if I have to get some ingredient for a recipe and it's not on sale. I'll search frantically for anything that boasts a discount; I'll even dare to ask the check-out clerk if she might have a coupon sitting around. And if not, crestfallen, I return to my house with my full-priced item, feeling like the dessert I'm making is worth more than gold.

I am the guru of garage sales, the yogi of yard sales, and the ruler of rummage sales. Suffice it to say I know how to package my junk, merchandise my crap, and glorify my cast-offs. My newspaper ads sound like I'm selling treasures from King Tut's tomb. When people show up at *my* sales, I can hawk with the best of them, and boy, do I know how to drive a hard bargain.

"Well," I say, "I don't know if I can come down on that. There was a lady here just 20 minutes ago and she's bringing her husband back to see it. You can buy it *now* for the full price, or I'll be happy to call you at the end of the day if it's still here." *Sold.*

I do try to be honest; I offer to let them plug in the electronics, I offer to let them open all the carefully wrapped packages of sheets or silverware. I offer to show them how something works, but mum's the word on the original price. After all, I got it for half-price or less so I'm selling it for how much I paid for it. And I always have a smile or a donut, whichever is needed for a hard sell.

After I've failed to sell all those items of irredeemable value that I no longer want (and apparently no one else does, either), I then schlep them to the resale shop. I have to split the profits 50/50 there, so it's my last resort. I work with a number of resale shops. They all have different criteria, and I know what will sell best at each store. I won't share my secret with you, so don't bother asking, but I will tell you that the end result is payment. A check comes every month like clockwork. It goes without saying, however, that all checks are not created equal, especially when dealing with resale shops. Some are smaller, some are larger, and none are for anywhere near what the items were worth in the first place. The most important thing is that they're out of my closet and that means room for more stuff to sell at the next rummage sale. My husband wonders why I even bother putting it in the closet. "Why not just take it right from Macy's to the resale shop?" he grumbles. A lot he knows. For Heaven's sake, I have to wear it at least once, decide that it doesn't look as good on me as I thought it did in the store, and then and only then can it go to one of the resale shops with clever names such as

Second Showing, *Once Removed*, or *Elite Repeat*. Each has its own unique specialty and each owner is looking for different things. Yes, I know where each item of mine will find the best home. It's a gift, what can I say? For instance, my wedding dress found a lovely temporary home at *Second to None*, where the owner priced it and sold it for me to someone eager to get a good deal. What? Did you think I should keep it? To wear on my 60th anniversary like my mother did? To clean house in it like my good friend Gladys did? No, you know me by now; I cleaned out my closet and made some money back on the purchase price (which in 1972 was $199). Do I split my profits with my husband? Absolutely not! That's my stash of gambling money, but, that'll have to be a topic for a different column.

Rummage sales are more profitable than the resale shops. I don't mind working hard, cleaning the garage, placing the ad and setting up the tables because I get the whole enchilada—every penny goes into my pocket, but those left-overs that even I would be embarrassed to take to a resale shop have to go somewhere, 'cause they're not going back into my house. It would be remiss of me to not give mention to Good Will, the Salvation Army and The White Elephant. If I just happen to be there dropping off multiple shirts, jackets and sweaters that I have spilled on, usually during the first wearing, then I have to wander through the aisles and peer at what goodies await. Perchance I might find something that fits into my myriad of collections of fish, roosters, Kachinas, salt and pepper shakers and lighthouses. After all, they are *cheap*.

My dad used to laugh at me. He called me *Second-hand Rose* because I always wanted the most bang for my buck. When my husband asked for my hand in marriage, my dad said, "Well, you'll never go broke with Bonnie. She knows how to shop." Poor Jim, he mistook that prophesy to mean that I would be a deliberate and careful shopper, watching pennies and spending wisely. Boy was he wrong!

Things That Go Beep in the Night

The other night we were awakened by the beeping of that most annoying appliance, the smoke alarm. We have smoke alarms in every room in the house just in case there is a smoker who sneaks in, sits on our davenport (for those of you who are imported to the Midwest, a davenport is a couch, only it takes longer to say it) while we are asleep and then falls asleep himself and his cigarette starts a fire. We also have carbon monoxide detectors. I'm not sure what they detect—I think people that come in the house with mono or maybe it's to detect if any of our guests get too monotonous. Then the detector buzzes and we send them home.

Back to my topic – being rudely awakened by an annoying noise telling us that a battery is dying. If only they would just perfect the dying battery so that it would just die instantly rather than performing a death scene to rival an opera diva performing Madam Butterworth. Because our ceilings are high, my poor husband has to get up (you didn't think I would get up, did you?), find his slippers and his glasses and then hover near each smoke alarm and carbon monoxide detector for as many minutes as it takes for the noise to repeat itself. After he finally identifies the bleepity-bleep offender he has to traipse into the garage for the ladder. By now I've pulled the pillow over my ears so the beeping does not disturb me or my dreams. I briefly consider getting up and holding the ladder for my dear hubby but I decide to roll over instead... well, until the alarm chirps again. One thing for sure, there cannot be a citizen in these United States who does not know exactly what is happening when they hear *that* beep in the middle of the night.

Compared to the tundra swans that arrive in the autumn and vacation by the Brownsville, Minnesota Overlook for weeks, the beeping of the batteries is nothing. We can hear those swans honking a mile away with our windows closed. It's not that noticeable in the day time – but the second your head hits that pillow, honk, honk, honk, honk. It must be the time that the swans conduct their town meetings. I'm pretty sure every swan talks at once and I don't know how they accomplish anything. I imagine that they are listening to weather reports and some are being filled in on flight patterns and the best motels along the route. Others are tired and want to remain for the winter and still others are just out on a date and want to be left alone to enjoy their swamp soup.

Have you ever had an invasion of the Minnesota State Bird— the mosquito? Naturally, it is impossible to keep those needle-nosed divers out of your bedroom and naturally they wait till you have turned off the lights and are just about asleep. Just as you drift off, BUZZZZZZZZZZZZZZZZ. Damn, you mutter. You lackadaisically swat around your head. BUZZZZZZZZZZZZZZ. Damn, you say. Go away. BUZZZZZZZZZZZZZZZZZZZ. Damn, you cry. Leave me alone. BUZZZZZZZZZZZZZ. Damn, you shout. Now you are out of bed, the lights are turned on and you are swatting at the air so frantically your poor husband cowers under the covers. Standing dead still you listen and watch. Looks like the coast is clear. Lights off. Slip between the sheets again. Whew. He's gone. Not your husband, just the mosquito. Peace. BUZZZZZZZZZZZZZZZZ.

Ever heard a screech owl? I have. In the middle of the night, of course. We listened to him night after night for a week. Where had he come from? Why was he here now? Was he going to take up residence on the top of the house next door forever? Finally, in anger and frustration I got up in the middle of the night to see where exactly he was perched.

I had my flashlight in hand and my robe securely fastened in case the neighbors happened to be looking out the window and my slippers on so I didn't step on a night crawler or a snake. Obviously my slippers would not stop me from stepping on them, but hopefully they would protect me from the yuckiness of squishing the former and being bit by the latter. I didn't turn on the outside light as I opened the door quietly and stepped on the sidewalk…oh no, I stealthily crept out and shined my flashlight into the peak of the log cabin next door and that's when it happened. I had the biggest scare of my life. There was this whooshing sound and a moving shadow the size of a Tyrannosaurus Rex created a breeze strong enough to blow my hair. I almost died as I dropped to the ground and scrambled, shivering, back into the garage. Apparently, through no fault of my own I believe, I must have frightened the owl and he abandoned his hide-out. He had a wing span of 100 feet I'm sure, and when he flew between the moon and me, I thought I was being attacked by Count Dracula. His screech was blood-curdling and the wind from his wings made this encounter with nature a bit too real. For those of you who know me, I prefer nature to stay outside as I observe it from inside. Therefore crickets and coyotes, which also make tons of noise mostly at night, are not on my list of favorite animals either.

 Just to prove that nothing good comes out of nighttime, have you gone to sleep with your windows open, a lovely summer breeze playfully teasing the sheer curtains over your windows and cooling you off from the day's heat as you realize that a sheet is all you need to cover up with? The night is peaceful, perfect, and suddenly, CRASH!! You bolt up from your slumber, your heart racing. What in the name of all that's holy was that? CRACK! You cringe from the flash of light that has illuminated your bedroom like a nighttime baseball game. It's only a storm, you realize. But wait. Was that predicted? No. How many windows did we leave open? Oh well, it doesn't matter. "Jim, go close all the windows. Please." You should always say "please" when you are trying to get someone to do an unpleasant chore for you.

About the Author

Bonnie Willemssen lives in Minnesota, but spends parts of the year in Arizona. Being retired has its advantages…lunching, playing Mahjongg, swimming, and writing. She began writing as a hobby in 2000 and found she had a gift for exaggeration packaged inside of a short story. From that kernel popped a second career—writing a humor column. At the insistence of her fans (there were at least ten or so), she collected the columns into *Rocky Road Is Not Just an Ice Cream* and now *Jack And Jill Are Over The Hill*. She is busy writing more columns, a book about finding her birth family, and completing the first book of a murder mystery series about a small town in Wisconsin. Join her Facebook page to get information of future releases of her books or to join her in person at one of her book signings.

Feel free to email her at bonniewillemssen@gmail.com or visit her on Facebook:

https://www.facebook.com/BonnieWillemssenAuthorPage

CPSIA information can be obtained
at www.ICGtesting.com
Printed in the USA
LVHW082055061222
734695LV00005B/607